The World Is
A
Prayerful Place

The World Is A Prayerful Place

Spirituality and Life

by

Dianne Bergant, CSA

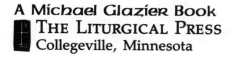

A Michael Glazier Book
THE LITURGICAL PRESS
Collegeville, Minnesota

A Michael Glazier Book published by the Liturgical Press

Cover design by David Manahan, O.S.B.

Copyright © 1987 by Michael Glazier, Inc.
Copyright © 1992 by The Order of St. Benedict, Inc., Collegeville, Minnesota. All rights reserved. No part of this book may be reproduced in any form or by any means, electronic or mechanical, including photocopying, recording, taping, or any retrieval system, without the written permission of The Liturgical Press, Collegeville, Minnesota 56321. Printed in the United States of America.

2   3   4   5   6   7   8   9

Library of Congress Cataloging-in-Publication Data

Bergant, Dianne.
    The world is a prayerful place / by Dianne Bergant.
        p.   cm.
    Originally published: Wilmington, Del. : M. Glazier, 1987.
    "A Michael Glazier book."
    ISBN 0-8146-5583-1
    1. Prayer. 2. Spirituality.   I. Title.
    BV210.2.B42   1991
    248.3'2—dc20   91-40842
                                                          CIP

CONTENTS

INVOLVEMENTS

DESTINIES

PREFACE

An attempt to write a book on prayer may be deemed an act of presumption. Consider the great classics on the subject. Who would dare to place oneself in the company of women and men of such caliber? And yet, if prayer is natural to human beings, another contemporary effort to provide a simple straightforward account of it is not only reasonable but could prove to be particularly valuable, valuable not in a utilitarian sense but in a contemplative sense.

The present book is offered not as a guide to prayer but as a reflection on it. It flows from the convergence of three different but interrelated currents of thought: a consideration of one's world view, meditation on the wisdom tradition of the biblical heritage, and a serious pondering of life itself. (The Introduction CURRENTS OF THOUGHT provides an elaboration of each of these three areas.) Only one aspect of this many-faceted experience called prayer is considered in this book, that is, prayer's "worldly" dimension. Since the wisdom tradition is a record of biblical Israel's encounter with life, major themes from this tradition seem especially appropriate for determining the parameters of reflection on prayer.

The chapters cluster around three major concerns about life: human origins, human relationships, and human destinies. Each reflection follows the same pattern: brief comments that flow from a perspective that is quite familiar to most readers; musings that proceed from a slightly different point of view; and finally, an invitation to readjust one's sights and to assume a new attitude toward the world and in prayer.

This book sets forth a way of looking at prayer that may be unfamiliar to some readers. Therefore, it may be helpful to explain how prayer is understood in this presentation before offering the prayerful reflections themselves.

A *Definition of Prayer*

"Prayer is the lifting of the mind and heart to God." Who has not heard that simple definition? Perhaps its very simplicity has become misleading and we have stifled the dynamism of the reality of prayer within the confines of a definition of it. Surely prayer is more than merely a lifting, even a lifting to God. Without denying the importance of prayer as an activity, we must look beyond mere performance or practice to discover the reality of prayer, a reality as varied in depth and expression as are the people who pray. No one description can possibly capture the totality of this phenomenon. The following reflections are offered as just one perspective. It may be new to some, and familiar to others, but it is a perspective that seems frequently to have been underestimated in popular considerations of prayer. It is a perspective that requires far greater attention and explicit treatment.

Prayer should be regarded more as an attitude toward life, the source of life, and the various manifestations of life than merely as a particular activity. It is a basic orientation toward reality that is first shaped by one's religious understanding and then reinforces that understanding in return. We usually begin to pray the way we have been taught to pray. Then, as we pray, we learn what prayer really is. Its underlying presuppositions are similar to, if not identical with, one's world view. A comparison with love might illustrate what is meant by this.

Prayer as an attitude toward life can be compared to love as an attitude toward another person. In a similar way, praying or the practices of prayer are more like acts of love or making love. In both instances, the latter actions flow from , are expressions of, and are indispensable to, the actual disposition but are not identical with it. Both love and prayer first presume and then deepen a relationship of reverence and intimacy. Thus, the manner in which one perceives one's partner in either of these relationships is fundamental to the way one lives and moves and breathes within such a partnership.

The reflections offered here build on two fundamental beliefs. First, God is our partner in prayer. Second, prayer is an attitude toward life, the source of life, and the various manifestations of life. The presupposition that underlies these two beliefs is that *God is manifested in life.* Thus, our attitudes toward life, that is, our worldview, significantly influence our attitudes in prayer.

Introduction

CURRENTS OF THOUGHT

World View

MASTERY OR HARMONY?

What seems to be today's prevailing world view or attitude toward life? By what criteria do we judge a person a "success"? What is the "pearl of great price" for which we seem willing to sacrifice all else in order to possess it? For many, life is a series of challenges, and people are judged according to their ability to meet these challenges and to emerge triumphant. For others, today's "pearl of great price" appears to be security, whether this is personal, economic or national. All of these views reflect a hidden predilection toward mastery. We are bent on conquering, conquering the secrets of the universe, the forces of nature, or any competitors in the fields of sports, industry, politics or international affairs. Once we have conquered, we devise elaborate systems of maintaining control lest we lose our positions of ascendancy. Having conquered and maintained sufficient control, we can then avail ourselves of whatever resources are at hand that might further our mastery.

These attitudes permeate our lives and influence our relationship with God. Over the years, various schools of devotion have espoused them. They exhort their followers to *control* unruly passions, to *overcome* evil desires, and to *withstand* the attacks of malevolent powers. In many instances, they strongly suggest that the material world is *at war* with the spiritual and must be *brought into submission*. Even prayer can reflect this point of view. One must *overcome* distractions and *fight* boredom. Only with *victory* can one hope for the coveted *prize* of contemplation.

What has been said about mastery *of* life, *in* life, or *in* prayer is all valid in a certain sense, but it is only one perspective. By itself it is a serious distortion, and it seems to be the prevailing distortion. An alternate point of view is offered here, a point of view that does not negate the values that have been described, but emphasizes a different approach to life. Stated simply this view insists: rather than adopt a posture of mastery, let us nurture an attitude of harmony. Let success be deemed in terms of cooperation, interdependence and mutuality. Even contemporary science and technology have brought us to realize that without these attitudes our very physical survival may be endangered, to say nothing of our political and international stability. We must begin to see that life can be neither exploited nor manipulated. It must be entered into cooperatively and lived deeply.

If prayer is understood as an attitude toward life, the source of life, and the various manifestations of life, then we must foster corresponding perspectives here as well. We must give up our habit of exploiting material creation for the sake of our piety and of attempting to manipulate God in the name of religion. We must enter into dialogue with reality and rediscover our affinity with the universe. Only then will these attitudes permeate our approach to everything.

RELATIONSHIPS

One of the most far-reaching accomplishments of the modern world is its insight into the significance of relationships. This realization is basic to our understanding of the sciences both physical and social. Newton's understanding of gravity was based upon this, as were Darwin's appreciation of the genetic unity of living things and Einstein's theory of relativity. Sociology and psychology have also uncovered the indispensiblity of healthy relationships for the survival and well-being of the individual and of the group. Meaningful human life is dependent upon wholesome enlivening relationships with others, with the rest of creation, with life itself, with God. The attitudes we have within one relationship will seldom be different from the attitudes we have within the others.

We are not born with attitudes, rather, we develop them. Much of this development escapes our consciousness and frequently we are unaware of the strength of our viewpoints as they become firmly rooted within us. These attitudes can be consciously fostered, however. We can be schooled by others or we can discipline ourselves in this process of development. For this to happen we must cultivate another habit, that of personal reflection.

We all engage in planning and judging, but how many people take the next step and try to understand why they do what they do? How many analyze their motivation in order to appreciate the origins of their behavior? How many realize the many influences on their thinking? This point is not meant as an indictment against the general public. However, a society that bombards us with a muliplicity of sensations does not usually encourage introspection. Therefore, we must take pains to develop the habit of personal reflection.

Upon what should we reflect? Upon our relationships! Our relationships with others; our relationships with the natural world; our relationships with God! Do we discover sentiments of love or disdain, compassion or indifference, justice or exploitation, peace or enmity? What kind of women and men are we? What kind of world view have we espoused? What kind of lives do we live? What kind of prayer do we pursue?

The Wisdom Tradition

The most widely held interpretation of the literary heritage of biblical Israel claims that this literature records the nation's testimony regarding God's involvement in the lives of the people and in their national history. Since most of the writing is narrative in form and since the arrangement of these stories suggests a kind of historical movement, it is clear why this view appears to be legitimate. However, not all of the biblical material fits into this category. There are didactic tales such as Ruth, Esther and Tobit which, although they contain historical elements, were probably intended as aids for teaching rather than as chronicles of history. The same is true with regards to the Psalms. They are replete with references to people and events of Israel's history, but their primary purpose was, and continues to be, liturgical rather than historical.

However, there is a particular category of biblical literature that seldom addresses Israel's distinctive relationship with God. Unlike most of the bible, its focus is anthropological rather than theological. It begins with the human and moves to the divine. This body of literature is known as the wisdom tradition.

The primary interest of the wisdom tradition is life and the successful living of it. Scholars are not in total agreement as to how this concept should be identified. While it is described in many different ways, the common idea running throughout all of the descriptions is the explicit concern for and appreciation of human dignity, human welfare, human values, human pursuits, and human success. The wisdom movement has been variously depicted as: a humanistic outlook on life, an ideology for coping with reality, a search for the underlying principles of casuality and order for the purpose of conforming to them, and an attempt to organize an otherwise chaotic existence. Each of these characterizations, though distinctly nuanced, agrees with the primary interest of the movement. Wisdom thinking speaks to appropriate attitudes toward life and attendant behavior that will result in happiness.

The primary source of wisdom is experience. This is not to suggest that practical knowledge automatically guarantees wisdom. We all know the adage, "No fool like an old fool!" Rather, astute reflection on experience can provide insight and understanding that can be attained by no other means. The wisdom tradition insists that extraordinary divine disclosure is not the only way we can come to know God. We encounter God *through* human experience not *in addition* to it, much less *despite* it. It is the experience of life that brings us to the threshold of mystery and prompts us to ask: What is the meaning of life? What is our place in the universe? What is the origin of the universe and what holds it together? Why do we suffer? What role, if any, does God play in human life? These are the questions addressed in the wisdom tradition. They are the perennial questions of life and they must be faced by every woman and man of every age in every culture regardless of religious orientation.

It should be clear that these questions originate from life itself and that no special pronouncement of religious teaching is required to mark their importance. The very probing of life's questions leads one to its mysterious and incomprehensible dimension. Although experiential wisdom may be within human grasp, often it seems that the longings of the human heart are really for something unattainable, something that transcends human bounds. The wisdom tradition provides encouragement and advice in this search for meaning and fulfillment.

THE ANCIENT VIEW OF REALITY

In order for us to comprehend the meaning and the implications of the perspectives which this tradition offers, a few words explaining the biblical concept of the universe might be helpful. The pre-scientific mind perceived reality as a three-leveled, interrelated collectivity. Recognizing regularity and relationships in the material world, the ancients of the Near East believed that the very same forces which were responsible for this order were also operative on a second level, human life and the social realm. These forces were deemed somehow divine and this property explained the stability of the two orders and their probable hierarchy. A natural order was recognized in the material world. Observing patterns of growth and movement as well as the effect of one physical body upon another, the ancients were able to discover some of the physical laws that govern the material world. They also designated certain habits of human behavior that promoted societal harmony and safeguarded peace. Furthermore, when this social order was threatened some form of juridical process was called upon to restore order. In addition to the natural and societal, a third order was proposed, a cosmic order. The ancients believed that the celestial bodies were divine or semi-divine and they made very little distinciton between the heavenly luminaries and the pantheon of the gods and goddesses. This cosmic order was understood as somehow divine. These three orders, the natural, the societal and the cosmic, constituted the ancient view of reality and the same laws of organization were thought to be operative within and among the orders. While Israel demythologized the cosmic order, it still accepted this basic view of reality.

RELATIONSHIPS OF INTERDEPENDENCE

Our advances in science have revealed the naivete of this understanding. The material world is not governed by moral standards, nor is behavior subject to physical laws. However, in spite of our dismantling of this perception of the universe, its fundamental concept remains well-grounded. There is a dynamic interrelationship operative within the universe that can be observed in different manifestations of interdependence. An example of this on one level would be the fact that the biosphere depends upon a delicate balance if life is to survive. As examples of this interdependence operative between levels we note that nonhuman creation either benefits or suffers from human decisions, and that, according to believers, somehow women and men are dependent upon the divine. The wisdom tradition, though operating out of this ancient world view of interdependence, can continue to provide insights for reflection as we in our contemporary world struggle with the perennial quesitons of life. A world view based on a concept of interrelationship is of supreme significance for our day.

Israel's system of order should not be understood as one of rigid determinism. Our religious ancestors had to struggle with contingency and ambiguity just as we do. Their science may have been naive but their insights into life certainly were not. In their search for meaning and security in life, they had to admit their inability to guarantee success. All they could hope for was the attainment of attitudes toward life that might enable them to make appropriate choices. And if in the process of choosing they discovered that they were in error, they hoped for wisdom to learn from the mistake and not repeat it. Wisdom did not enable them to eliminate ambiguity, but to deal with it. Life was as unpredictable for them in the past as it is for us in the present. While some people then thought, and some people today think, that life can be controlled, the wise knew and continue to know that such is not the case. Life can only be lived.

The Questions of Life

Life poses so many questions that seem to have no enduring answer. At every turn, beyond every horizon, we are confronted with issues we thought we had resolved, with challenges we were sure had been met. And such probably was the case. We would not be able to turn corners nor reach horizons had we not dealt with pressing issues. The truth of the matter is that the fundamental questions and challenges of life are always at least one step ahead of us, forever demanding our attention and calling us forward. Our answers and our solutions are only provisional at best. Realizing this, any one of us can find life overwhelmingly frustrating or endlessly exciting depending upon our point of view. If life is seen as a series of tasks to be accomplished, then the drive for success can produce unimagined tensions and past performance is no guarantee to future fulfillment. On the other hand, if the moment by moment experience of living is what is cherished, then we must bring to bear on that moment everything that we are, and live it to the best of our ability, moving gracefully to the next moment and to the next and to the next.

Regardless of how we perceive life, we will always have to face questions of meaning or futility, of success or failure, of power or weakness, of happiness or misery, of life or death, questions that occupied the sages of Israel. The way we deal with these questions at one time and in one situation may be quite different from the way we deal with them at another. There is no predetermined pattern to follow; no set of answers to memorize and then apply when opportune. The only way to acquire a facility for living is by really living. This demands a realistic sense of who we are, what we have, and what we are about.

Perhaps the best way to begin our reflections on life is to take a good look at ourselves. How are we made? Of what are we made? What makes us tick? If we stand in relationship with the material world, with others, and with God, what is at the heart of each relationship? What are the responsibilities? What are the consequences? The wisdom tradition provides some very interesting insights into these questions. The creation narratives in Genesis 1 and 2 may be scientifically naive, but the anthropology there is profound. The early worshippers of our God acknowledged human affinity with the elements of the earth, while at the same time recognizing that there is a dimension of this earth-creature that transcends the purely material. Their anthropological perspective included some thought about the relationship between the sexes as well. All of this, along with a testimony of a faith in the divine creator, is found in the creation accounts.

Some believers contend that nature itself exercises a mysterious power over humans and they explain this power as akin to the divine. Is our search for more and more understanding really a search for God? Is God appealing to us through nature? From within nature? Contrary to what some religious systems have claimed, nature is neither debased nor demonic. The biblical tradition states that "God saw that it was good!" In the story of Noah it also claims that nature is in covenant with God. Clearly, our attitude toward nature flows from our understanding of our relationship with it.

It makes little difference where we begin our reflections on life, since all of them impinge upon how we understand God and our relationship with God. The biblical tradition depicts

God as wise and powerful creator, just and merciful savior, loving mother and father. It also insists on God's transcendance, incomprehensibility, and ineffability. Sometimes it questions the justice of God, the providence of God, the trustworthiness of God. At times, these characterizations of God have been very helpful in our struggle to articulate our experience of God, at other times they have proven to be a hindrance. We too have questioned our conceptions of God. We know the skepticism of Qoheleth as well as the agonizing dilemma of Job. The way we ask our questions and the way we answer them will be influenced by our attitudes toward life, the source of life, and the various manifestations of life.

ORIGINS

OF WHAT ARE WE MADE?

Then the Lord God formed the earth-creature
of the dust of the ground, and breathed
into its nostrils the breath of life;
and the earth-creature became a living being.

Genesis 2:7

Then God said, "Let us make humankind
in our image, after our likeness;"

Genesis 1:26a

Of what are we made? It is common practice within certain circles to pose that question, but how often do we peer beneath the surface of the question and probe the depths of the answer? Perhaps it takes the marvel of newborn life or the mystery of recent death to awaken us to the wonders of human existence.

Of what are we made? The way we answer the question depends largely upon our world view. If we do not believe that there is a spiritual dimension to human existence, we will answer in purely materialistic terms. If we are women and men of faith, our answers will reflect our religious tradition.

We are made of body and soul! Dust of the earth and the breath of life! Matter and a spark of the divine!

The book of Genesis offers us two different statements about creation. While these two theologies originate from different periods of biblical Israel's history and in response to different religious concerns, the views of humankind of the two traditions are very similar. We are creatures of the earth as are the fish of the sea, the birds of the air, the cattle and every creeping thing that creeps on the earth (Gen 1:26-28). We were formed from the earth as were the rest of living things (Gen 2:7, 9, 19). However, unlike the rest of creation, there is a dimension to humankind that transcends the stuff of the earth. The Priestly writer called it the image/likeness of God (Gen 1:26-27). The earlier Yahwist spoke of the breath of life (Gen 2:7). We are a mysterious composite of material and immaterial. Our understanding of this combination has shaped our values, ordered our priorities, influenced our conception of the purpose of life, and played a significant role in the way we pray.

From the Dust of the Earth

All are from the dust, and all
return to dust again.

Ecclesiastes 3:20

We are made of the dust of the earth. Somewhere along our journey through history apparently we began to disdain this material side of our being. We resented the demands made upon us by our bodies. The interrelationship between the material and the immaterial deteriorated into antipathy and we found that we were at war with ourselves. According to one religious insight, this world and the things of this world which exerted such a pernicious influence over us had to be subjugated to the power of the spirit. It seemed that only prayer for mastery of the body, accompanied by penance and discipline, could check our propensity for self-indulgence.

Anyone who embarked on a life of prayer was well acquainted with the resistance set up by the body. Fatigue, discomfort of every kind, and distractions all joined together to wage war against spiritual aspirations. Programs of discipline were devised to develop habits intended to keep "the flesh" in check. All of our energies were devoted to the mastery of the "baser" side of our nature.

There is no denying the power of human appetite and sensation. Unchallenged and misdirected they can wreak havoc in the lives of individuals and in society at large. However, unlike the rest of material creation, we are seldom satisfied with mere survival. We strive for a quality of life that transcends the level of existence enjoyed by the rest of the world around us, while at the same time we feel a strong attraction to and kinship with this world. We feel torn in opposite directions, confronted by an existential dilemma, compelled to decide in favor of one dimension of our nature at the expense of the other. This dualistic perception pervades our entire world view, our relationship with the rest of creation, and our manner of prayer.

Indeed, there *is* more to life than the material world around us, and the human person has higher aspirations than mere conquest of this world. "What is essential is invisible to the eye."

HOWEVER . . . As we stand within the mystery of life and gaze with wonder at what is, we realize that we can discover what is essential only by first seeing with the eye, hearing with the ears, feeling with all the sensitivity of the body. Our physical powers are far from inconsequential, much less are they base. We would do well to rediscover our affinity with the world and learn to live in harmony with it, rather than to perpetuate an unnecessary and undesirable sense of enmity toward it. Perhaps thereby we can touch again that sacred center of being that links every thing to every other thing.

We are truly children of the universe, made of the same stuff as are the mountains and the rain, the sand and the stars. We are governed by the laws of life and growth and death as are the birds and the fish and the grass of the field. We thrive in the warmth of and through the agency of the sun as does every other living thing. We come from the earth as from a mother, and we are nourished from this same source of life. We are creatures of the earth and so we shall always be. How can we possibly despise this very basic dimension of our being and hope to live in peace with God who made us thus? Have we forgotten the biblical statement of divine approval: "And God saw that it was good"?

At some mysterious moment eons ago the cosmic process reached a point of development where matter took shape in living forms. Billions of years later, these living forms developed levels of consciousness until the fullness of consciousness appeared in humankind. Thus, we are a form of life reflecting upon itself. In a sense, we are the consciousness of creation, but we do not thereby cease to be corporeal.

We are not only witnesses to the miracles of life, we are participants in them. They take place within us, within our bodies. We take into these bodies elements of the inanimate world and we transform them into living substance, into our own animate being. It is through our bodies that life is passed on from generation to generation. We do not create life; we transmit it; and we do this through bodies made of the dust of the earth. Surely this is not base. It is awesome!

We alone, of all material reality, stand in the midst of the world, conscious of the glories of creation—of which we are but one manifestation. We alone can allow this consciousness to well up within us, to permeate us, and to spill over into that total fascination with reality known as contemplation. We cannot extricate ourselves from the world of which we are a part. We must be absorbed in its wonders, amazed by its beauty, and stand in awe of that wisdom and power behind it that we call God.

If we value our corporeal being in this way, we will realize that our bodies with their yearnings and powers need not be obstacles to prayer. They are our only way of being of and in this world. They are a means of the expression of life. Like everything else about us, they are what we are and what we have from God. Of themselves they may be useless; by themselves they could be harmful; but as an integrated component of the composite that we are—a composite of material and immaterial—they are marvelous and awe-inspiring.

The sights and sounds, flavors and aromas of the world attach us to people, places and events of life. At first they inundate us with their impressions and then, at a later date, they invade the corridors of our memories calling back those experiences and the circumstances that made them memorable. Without denying the need for personal harmony, one wonders about the meaning of "mortification of the senses."

The idea presupposes a corruptive power that must be quelled by self-denial. In reality these senses are not only attuned to our world, but they are the means whereby we participate in this world, thus bringing creation to the threshold of contemplation.

THEREFORE, as we reach into the recesses of our being, and touch the forces of life within us, we can experience again the pristine exhilaration of living. We can discover the pulse of the universe in the pattern of our own heartbeat, and the ebb and flow of life in the rhythm of our breathing. We can stand humble and speechless in face of the privilege of being a part of the universe, of being a thread in the vast network of life, of being an expression of conscious vitality. Through our corporeal being, we can bring material creation to the contemplation of the source of all that is.

In order to find real meaning in life let us live in harmony with it. To live in harmony with the world is to live in harmony with the creator of the world, and this is the only attitude that can dispose us for that communion that we call prayer. We cannot resent our commonality with what is material and passing, for that is to question divine wisdom and benevolence and will only result in a sense of frustration and futility. For it is not that we *have* bodies and that they must be controlled; we *are* bodies. Enspirited bodies. Conscious bodies. Bodies that can flourish and survive only in an atmosphere of harmony and interdependence. Bodies that can enter into dialogue with the universe and with the ineffable God.

There Is a Time for Everything

A time to weep and a time to laugh;
A time to mourn and a time to dance.

Ecclesiastes 3:4

The world view that disparages whatever is material probably will entertain a fundamental distrust of human emotion
and yearning as well. The passions and desires meant to be
expressions of our personalities and to serve as prods in our
strivings will be despised, because unchecked they open the
doors to every manner of selfishness and violence. So many
times we find ourselves not only incapable of harnessing the
power of emotion, but unable to understand its origin and
intensity. We may contend that emotions are in themselves
neutral, but we are well aware of the reprehensible behavior
that frequently flows from them.

Who has not been the victim of another's anger, hatred or
jealousy? Greed has enslaved whole societies; lust has des-
troyed families; and self-pity has eaten away the determination of countless people. It seems that passion and not principle is the motivating force in the lives of many. Even those
who make every effort to adhere to religious values often fall
short of their ideals. They may succumb to feelings of melan-
choly, resentment, and even antagonism. They may know rage
and immorality as well as apathy and despair. Indeed, unruly
emotions often deprive us of the happiness and fulfillment
that life can offer.

In addition to this, our society has conceived profiles
outlining which emotions are acceptable for women and men
respectively. Part of the socialization of the individual has
been the appropriation of these predetermined characteris-

tics. For example, aggression, independence and sexual desire, indispensable in men, are deemed unacceptable in women. Conversely, women are conditioned to be docile, tender and self-effacing, yet these attitudes are scorned in men. Deviation from these norms often results in social reproach. One must conform if one is to be considered a well-adjusted individual.

It becomes increasingly clear that emotional maturity is essential for one's well-being and for the welfare of society. This maturity can only be achieved by adhering to reasonable personal and societal standards and by developing habits of self-discipline. The emotions must be bridled and brought under control.

ON THE OTHER HAND . . . Emotion is the way we respond to the experiences of life. It not only enhances living, but it can also help us to differentiate between what is desirable and what is repulsive, what might be beneficial and what might be harmful, what should be pursued and what should be avoided. Feelings are clues to our interests, our inclinations, our values. While they should not regulate our lives, neither should they be banished from them.

FEAR

How could we survive without fear? We are fragile, vulnerable beings. There are so many things that can hurt us, that can endanger our lives. The forces of nature show no partiality toward human nobility. We can be crushed or swept away like a stone or a branch of a tree. We can become the prey of animals or the victims of disease. We can be shattered by another human being—neglected or despised, exploited or physically harmed. We fear for our lives, our safety, our well-being; and so we protect ourselves. We avoid, as best we can, whatever threatens our security. But eventually we reach a point where we know that there is no ultimate defense. We are vulnerable; we will always be vulnerable because we are mortal. Fear can ignite the survival instinct within us but it can also bring us to an acknowledgement of the limits of our creaturehood.

In the face of this, what can a fragile human being do? Trust! It was the mystery that we call God that drew us into life in the first place. This same mystery engulfs us and sustains us, and it is in its presence that we must stand with hearts and minds full of confidence. True, we are vulnerable and consequently fearful, but this vulnerability proceeds from our very nature and the consequent fear can open us to trust in God, the architect of that nature.

GRIEF

One of the most consuming emotions to grip the human heart is sadness. It can come upon us unexpectedly when our hopes are dashed and we long for what might have been. It can intrude upon us when the accomplishments for which we worked so hard are snatched from our grasp, or when the people with whom we knit our lives are torn from our embrace. Disillusionment, failure and death all give rise to a boundless emptiness known as grief. Plan as we may we are not prepared for it, nor can we escape it when it arrives. It is no respecter of persons. In fact, it seems to be cruellest to the most sensitive.

Sorrow is inevitable in a world of contingency and transience. We invest ourselves in our dreams. The disillusionment that springs from unfulfilled hopes and the sense of failure that often immobilizes us are the residue of this investment. Nothing in life is certain; nothing lasts; and still we hope and dream and strive.

Perhaps even more instinctively we attach ourselves to people. Imperceptibly we weave our lives together with others in such a way that, though separation creates a void that will not be filled, the bonds that unite us are really not severed. We live with grief and the sense of loss, knowing that something of what we had cannot be taken from us, and we are willing to make the same commitment again if given the chance.

It is imperative that we open ourselves to this emotional involvement regardless of the sorrow that may accompany it. Our hopes and dreams are what inspire us. The risk of disappointment is a small price to pay for having a purpose in life. And how can we begin to measure the value of human affection? Commitment to others and personal involvement in their lives is in reality the most worthwhile pursuit we can undertake. The pain we are willing to endure for our attachment is clear evidence of our devotion. It can bring us to our knees before God whose tenderness made our commitment possible in the first place, and who will not withdraw that tenderness from us. Familiarity with sorrow marks a heart that has hoped and that has loved, a heart like the heart of God.

JOY

Despite its unavoidable predicaments, life still holds an indefinable something that runs throughout it like a mysterious stream. It is like a breeze on a summer evening or a firefly at night. It delights and escapes and delights again, able to tease us only when it is free. It is in the wonder of a baby who is charmed by a shadow's playful dance on a wall. It is in the rapture of one who is transported on the crescendo of a symphonic movement. It is in the serenity of a couple basking in the sunset of an evening or in the sunset of life. This indefinable something can only be called the joy of living.

Each one of us discovers this joy in different ways, at different times, in different places. It darts to and fro, tantalizing us with its mischief and holding us with its magic. We are always in search of it. At times we find it. But even then it cannot be commanded; it can only be savored.

What is it in life that can provoke laughter or a simple smile? What is it that touches a chord within us releasing gaiety and lightheartedness? Surely we were meant to dance and sing and rejoice. This must have been God's intent for there is so much in life that elicits such response. And even when happiness seems beyond our grasp, our yearning and striving for it attests to its fundamental importance in our lives.

Denigrating the pleasures in life is no way of showing approval of and appreciation for God's designs. However, a heart that exalts in the sheer joy of living cannot be far from praise of God's grandeur and gratitude for God's favors. Intoxication with life often breaks forth into paeans to the divine source of that life.

LOVE

From our earliest awakenings of personality until death puts an end to our earthly pursuits, we cry from the very center of our being for that mysterious exchange known as love. We open to it as a delicate mountain blossom opens to the warmth and vitality of the sun. We are transformed by the inner dynamism it awakens. We are invigorated by the hidden sources of life it taps. We are sustained and challenged by it, caressed and consoled. We come to life by the love of others and we quicken life within them by our love. It is a mutual miracle. By loving we fashion each other into tender, sensitive women and men.

Love has been the motivating force behind the most sublime actions of human history. It has inspired generosity, fidelity and heroism and given birth to art, music and poetry. Mothers and fathers have gazed with wonder and adoration into a blanket of squirming life. Lovers have been so captivated with each other that the rest of the world fades into the shadows. The love of friends and compatriots has sometimes superseded the love of life itself. Something within the human heart reaches out to what is beautiful, what is honorable, what is true, and we give of ourselves irrespective of the cost. Love calls us out of ourselves, out of our securities into the unknown terrain of commitment. It is a terrible risk! We could be wrong; we could be fools; we could be rejected! But still we take the risk, for we believe the adage; "It is better to have loved and lost, than never to have loved at all."

Only those who have tried to love can really try to pray. Only those who have been willing to stand open and defenseless before another, can stand open and defenseless before *the* other. For while it is true that love transforms and invigorates, sustains and challenges, caresses and consoles us, we know that it is really God who does this. And we know that as we stand in prayer before God, we bring the very same hearts that have been touched and enlivened by human love.

AND SO, let us embrace life with all of the emotion of which we are capable. Rather than haggle over the cost, let us seize the moment and all that it offers for it may not come again. Life is too dear merely to survive in it. The hopes and dreams born within the human heart are too precious to be squandered. The only thing that really matters is people, our attachment to them, our love for them. To live without commitment, without involvement, without emotion is really not to live at all. But to move through life passionately, yet tenderly, touching all within our reach, to test the limits of our humanness and know the intensity of its response, to experience every dimension of life and be grateful for the opportunity is to be fully alive and thereby to give glory to God.

A Little Less than the Angels

O Lord, you have searched me and you
know me. You know when I sit and when
I stand. You understand my thoughts
from afar.

Psalm 139:1-2

We are made in the image and according to the likeness of God. But what does this mean? Is that explanation correct which claims that a spark of the divine enlivens us and is ceaselessly striving to be released from the confines of our material bodies in order to be reunited to God? Or are we like God in that we possess a supernatural component similar to yet different from the divine essence? Is this image/ likeness perhaps a godly faculty? Or does it refer to a divine-like function? Is the image the same as the likeness? Or are they two different phenomena? These questions have been answered in countless ways over the ages and, regardless of the divergence of the answers advanced, they all seem to agree on one point. There is a dimension to humankind that transcends the stuff of the earth.

While we are a mysterious composite of the material and the immaterial, it often seems that our most immediate experience and our strongest impressions are related to the material world of which we are a part. This is not to suggest that our spiritual abilities lie dormant during most of our lives, but rather that it seems easier to be conscious of our physical needs and interests than of the immaterial dimension of our being. This latter dimension requires deliberate cultivation and refinement in a way that our bodies do not. The survival instinct that we have in common with so much of the rest of the animate world provides significant opportunity for physical growth and development. Some have concluded from this that the spiritual powers far excel those of the body and, therefore, should be preferred over them.

There is no doubt that humankind possesses certain superior abilities. Both the creation account of Genesis 1 and the current theory of evolution claim that humankind is the highest living form to have appeared. Yet these superior powers are the very powers that frequently lead to heinous behavior. Arrogance and inordinate pride in our intelligence are no strangers to the human consciousness. They usually lead to disdain for the less intellectual and to a kind of discrimination in society. In addition to those decisions that are truly wise, some of our other judgments unfairly consign individuals and groups to the fringes of our attention and concern. Memory is invaluable, but we also store up impressions that can eat away at our reasonableness and result in distortion, prejudice or hatred. Our creativity has often been directed toward devising systems of oppression, violence and destruction and then providing rationalization for their employment. Sins of this nature are far more insidious than the "weaknesses of the flesh." We must be wary of the powers of the mind. With all of their excellence they can be sinister. Indeed, they have been regarded as being the real cause of our downfall. According to the most widely held interpretation of the Fall narrative, it was pride that resulted in the expulsion of our ancestors from the garden. And pride has been at the heart of every serious offense since that time. There is no doubt that a misuse of our spiritual faculties has repeatedly alienated us from others and from God.

AND YET . . . It is by means of these very powers that we are lifted above the rest of creation to levels of consciousness far beyond our imagining. There we can gaze upon the rest of the world with reverence and not disdain. We can recognize our primacy and then realize the responsibility that accompanies it. As images of God, we stand in the midst of creation able to do what no other creature can do. We can think and decide. We can imagine and remember. We can consciously praise God.

THOUGHT

We have only begun to discover the depths of the human mind. We know; and we know that we know. The forms and flavors, the textures and aromas, the timbres and shades of reality that we perceive are not merely objects that impinge upon our consciousness. They have meaning and purpose and a place in our world. We can discover that meaning and discern that purpose and recognize that place. We can know; we can understand; we can stand in admiration of the marvels of this creation and the awesomeness of the creator.

The human mind has searched the microcosm of molecular structure and the macrocosm of the galaxies. There is no area of the physical universe that has not been the subject of intense and persistent inquiry. As is appropriate for children with questioning minds, we have been thrilled when the secrets of creation unfold before us. The more we uncover, the more we probe. By careful and respectful observation, we discover the order and regularity of the universe and some of its governing laws. Nature, which once appeared so threatening, is becoming intelligible. We are recognizing anew the interrelatedness and interdependence of all material forms.

Not satisfied with looking outward, we have turned our penetrating gaze on our own inner depths. We have become fascinated with the workings of our minds. We seek to understand human motivation and response as well as the way all of the mental faculties operate. We never cease to be amazed at the created wonder that we are. We can associate and differentiate; we can compare and contrast; we can elaborate and summarize; we can speculate and revise; and we can communicate both what we are doing and the results of what we have done. The human mind seems to be insatiable in its quest for knowledge and understanding.

The questions that we ask of reality include not only "What?" and "How?" but also "Whence?" and "Why?" They are questions that lead to the origin and purpose of the universe, questions that lead to the creator. Something of God calls to us from creation and we are compelled to pursue it. We have never been satisfied with mediocre answers but rather have pushed toward ultimate explanations. We know that we cannot attain them but we press on nonetheless. The inquiring mind brings us to the mystery behind creation, to the mysterious creator of all. Having arrived in our search at that point where we know that we stand before the immensity of God, we plunge headlong into this divine reality, seeking even the slightest insight into its irresistible attraction and mystery. We yearn to know about God. Indeed, we yearn to know God. The workings of the human mind have opened the door to contemplation.

DECISION

Another one of the marvelous powers that we enjoy is the ability to decide. We are not coerced into moving in predetermined directions. We are free, and how we glory in our freedom. We insist on it. We are willing to suffer and, if need be, even die to preserve it. Because we are free, we can ponder various options and make our own choices. This means that the future is never really preordained. It is full of possibilities, full of newness. Because we are free, we can exercise limitless originality as we fashion our very lives. We can follow fresh insights and devise creative ways to allow them to flourish. We have so much to say about the kind of people we will be and about the kind of world in which we will live. No other creature can freely exercise such influence. Because we are free, we can choose for or against what is good and true, what is of value and of integrity. Any choice which we make serves to enhance its value. It shows that we not only recognize its importance but that we desire it as well.

True, there is risk in the exercise of this faculty. We can make mistakes. Because of human limitations we can settle for less than we should. We can even choose what is worthless and harmful. But the ability to decide is a treasure the value of which far surpasses any risk involved. It is a faculty that can bring us face to face with creaturehood in a unique way. If we are mistaken and our decisions prove to be erroneous, we can acknowledge our error. We can admit our human failings and stand humbly before God, conceding that we are but amateurs in the art of living. Our mistakes, if seen in the right light, can help us to "become again as little children," confessing our dependence upon God, a dependence out of which we will never grow. Caught up in the euphoria of self-direction and free choice, we can still accept the parameters that creaturehood imposes upon us and be content to exercise our decision-making faculty in a limited fashion.

In addition to this, while it is true that all of creation—and this includes humankind—comes from God and tends toward God for fulfillment, we alone have the ability consciously to accept this and live in harmony with it. We alone can follow the biblical injunction to "Choose life!" We alone can proclaim that we not only need God, but want God. Although the power to choose may be limited, it is magnificent nonetheless. It enables us freely to enter into a loving relationship with the ineffable God and to shape our lives accordingly.

CREATIVITY

Somewhere within every one of us is the spark of creativity. It manifests itself in as many different ways as there are people. It explains the originality in the way we perceive, or think, or express ourselves, or arrange things around us. And the fruits of creativity delight the human spirit. At times this spark seems carefree and impetuous, surprising us with its inspiration. Then it sinks deep into the fiber of our being producing a warmth and glow that is constant and sustaining. At other times it smolders within us only to flash forth with an intensity that is unrestrained and all-consuming.

How else can we explain the silent welling-up of the melodic waves that eventually crash upon the consciousness of those of us endowed with musical ability? The melody, the harmony, the orchestration originate from hidden recesses that not even the musician can identify. It is somehow within the person ebbing and flowing, surging forward and then receding until it takes shape in smoothly flowing sound, that thrills the human spirit and lifts it above the tawdry and mundane.

Those of us who cannot compose music can be enraptured by its beauty. It can stir within us sentiments long standing or newly discovered. It can inspire hope and courage in the despairing, soothe and comfort those sick at heart, or awaken the sources of vitality dormant within us. Music is truly the "harmonious voice of creation; an echo of the invisible world."

Creativity also explodes into profusions of color and texture and form. The ability to blance light and shadow and tone and hue, the versatility in working with patterns and creating designs, and the skill in conveying the impression of depth and perspective all contribute to the making of an artist. Such creativity cannot be learned; it is innate. It can only be cultivated and refined. When expressed, it draws our attention to something within the created world, and then, by means of media and style, speaks of beauty and truth and human aspiration.

We stand and gaze in admiration at works of art. We are spellbound by the inventiveness and flair of one piece and the understated artistry of another. We marvel at the diversity of ideas and execution and yet the commonality of theme. Each creation expresses some aspect of human experience. The artist has taken the substance of the material world and, like the potter-God of the biblical narrative, has formed something new, something that lives through the spirit of life expressed within it.

Probably the most universal display of creativity is found in human thought. New insights, new ideas, new understandings come to all of us. The resulting conclusions that we draw and the influences that they have upon our lives are contributing factors to the emergence of our individuality. Yet they are not so unique as to be incommunicable. We benefit from, indeed we thrive on, the creative thinking of others. It is the origin of science and technology. It is also the origin of poetry, drama and humor. There is little significant human striving or accomplishment ever conceived in the mind of any one of us and preserved in writing that has not resonated in the depths of other women and men, who have known the same stirrings but have not articulated them so creatively.

The selection and arrangement of words in such a way as to allow our thought to run freely down the paths of imagination not only spring from creative insight but give rise to it as well. The ability of one to capture the poetry of life in language and imagery nourishes the poetic sensitivities of others. Likewise, the magnitude and scope of emotion that is unleashed in a dramatic presentation pay homage to the talent of the writer. Yet this is true only insofar as the work voices fundamental human truths, truths that are found in every human soul. The literary artist is one who can fashion dynamic and penetrating expressions out of the clay of linquistic forms.

It has been said that one of the ways we are distinguished from the other animals is that we can see the humor in life and we can laugh at it. We all have this capacity, but some of us possess a special talent of wit. These know when to exaggerate and when to minimize, and thus cast the situation into ridiculous light. Jesters, clowns and mimes have all brought lightheartedness and laughter into lives that are laced with pain and tragedy. Their gentle harmless nudging has often assisted us in putting things in the right perspective. In laughing at these we discover that we are laughing at ourselves. What a comic does by means of performance, a punster or humorist does with words. In ingenious ways they all dismantle our categories and disarm us while at the same time encourage us to fashion and reform.

Is it any wonder that people frequently understand the image/likeness in terms of human creativity? It is such an astounding ability that we have—an ability possessed by no other creature—that we think of it as a mysterious human participation in divine creative power. However we understand it, we cannot but be overwhelmed by our ability to conceive of such splendor and profundity. In some small way we imitate the music, artistry and interiority of creation. We are surely marvels of the creativity of God.

MEMORY

Finally, memory is the treasury of our past. There a record of our life is preserved, ready to be brought to consciousness by the slightest suggestion. The colors and brilliance of Christmases long past can warm our hearts again, as can the carefree beach fires and homecoming rallies of the good old days. The familiar smiles of children who are now graying, and the kindness in eyes that have long since closed, can carry us back to times that played their part in shaping us into the people we have become. We can live in the glow of a vibrant and sustaining love, able to travel in memory through its most treasured moments and relive its first innocence and devotion. All of this is possible because we can remember.

Knowledge and civilization are built on the accomplishments of the past. Systems of thought proceed from one idea to another, retaining unchanged some of what was affirmed earlier, refining what still has meaning, and abandoning what no longer has relevance. Without memory and the ability to move the past into the present, every generation would have to rediscover fire and reinvent the wheel. Instead, we inherit the wealth of the ages, contribute to these treasures, and bequeath an enriched legacy to the next generation. All of this is possible because we can remember.

We cherish a religious heritage, the heart of which is a calling to mind God's saving action of the past. We are people of the covenant whose liturgical celebration is a continual renewal of this commitment. We are fashioned, sustained, inspired and spurred on by written and oral traditions which originated at another time, in another culture, but which have been safeguarded in the religious memory of a believing community. This heritage serves to unite us with our religious ancestors thus establishing an unbroken thread of faith. All of this is possible because we can remember.

THIS BEING THE CASE, let us follow our inquiring inclinations and rejoice in the abilities that flow from our nature. As the voice of the universe calls out to us, let us continue to explore its secrets in order to lay bare, as best we can, the treasures of creation. As we probe and uncover, test and conclude, we will be able to enter even more deeply into the inner workings of the world. With our finely tuned minds we can trace these movements and follow them ever more deeply into as yet unexplored regions. We can find God! As wisdom calls out to us and the voice of understanding is raised, we can ascend the heights that stretch above the paths we have been following. We can enter into the house that wisdom has built, and feast at the table of understanding.

Let us be resolute as we journey through life encountering the myriad forks in the road. Shall we turn to the left or to the right? Shall we follow wisdom or folly? We should not vacillate; we must decide. Let us trust in the basic goodness of our nature and rely on God's compassion towards our mistakes. The notion of freedom embraces the possibility of error. This ever-present possibility is what makes our decisions so heartening and meaningful. In the face of many possibilities we continue to choose in favor of each other, to choose in favor of life, to choose in favor of God.

Every day provides a fresh beginning to life, an opportunity to give birth to new ideas and new hopes, a chance to revivify the world with new beauty and new spirit. Human ingenuity can no more be stamped out than can the artistry of God, for it springs from this artistry. And so, let us never cease to rejuvenate the world, a world weary and worn. We can touch the life force hidden in its bosom, and call it back to vitality and gaiety. We can paint the world with clean and honest colors, fill it with the pure tones of invigorating music, and cause it to burst forth with laughter at its own foibles. "We know that the whole creation has been groaning in travail together until now." We can bring this creation to new birth, for we participate in the creative activity of God.

And finally, let us never forget! Let us never forget the tenderness and unselfishness we have received from others. Let us never forget our kinship with and dependence upon the earth. Let us never forget the lessons we have learned from the past. Let us never forget the loving kindness of God that has accompanied us at every moment of life. Gratitude inundates the heart that remembers. Gratitude and humility and sensitivity and wisdom. Such a heart is prepared for prayer. Such a heart is open to contemplation.

Our Hearts are Restless

> Wisdom speaks: I love those who love me, and those who seek me diligently find me. Riches and honor are with me, enduring wealth and prosperity.
>
> *Proverbs* 8:17-18

The story of human history is more than a tale of survival. It is a record of aspirations engendered in the human heart, of goals set and strategies devised to achieve them, of magnificent accomplishments and dismal failures, and of an indefatigable determination to continue. Civilizations have been born and have matured as a result of this ambition and diligence. They have also been conquered and enslaved when these same dispositions have been mustered against them. While we recognize the legitimacy of human aspirations and desires, we are all too well acquainted with the aberrations that can and do occur here.

The innate human need for satisfaction and fulfillment has often been promoted. As a result, every form of overindulgence has sooner or later been tolerated and even fostered. Happiness, our ultimate goal in life, has frequently been replaced by immediate excitement and shortlived pleasure. The advantages of success and prosperity sometimes seem to far outweigh the standards and principles of honesty that should guide us in our pursuits. In a world where the fundamental social structure appears to be economic, and judgments are made on the basis of material value, human achievement is tantamount to amassment and consumption. One occasionally questions the fundamental integrity of human ambition.

Although our biblical heritage does not espouse an anthropology that holds humankind in contempt, nonetheless, it has always readily acknowledged human iniquity. This moral failure has often been explained as the inevitable consequence of a fallen nature, a nature that can no longer be trusted. Such distrust is behind much of the exhortation to virtue that has become a part of religious devotion. Mortification and self-denial are thought to be the only way to curb one's lust for pleasure, while humiliation and self-depreciation are necessary in order to stifle pride in one's accomplishments. Life itself has been disparaged and has been called a 'vale of tears,' a kind of testing that must be endured before one can enter into 'real' life.

The inevitability of human error and even infamy cannot be denied. Human aspirations can be jaded and human ambition rapacious. Our desires appear to be insatiable and our self-reliance arrogant. Personal discipline and humility are indeed indispensable for harmonious living.

HOWEVER THAT MAY BE . . .

FULFILLMENT

The unquenchable drive of the human spirit and its efforts toward excellence bespeak a vitality and natural disposition that demand our respect. Our striving for satisfaction and fulfillment is more than mere egotistical grasping. It comes from a hunger within us that is never completely appeased. We are like the sea, open to the emptying rivers yet never filled by them. We are always thirsting for more—more beauty, more goodness, more truth. We never seem satisfied to rest in what we have accomplished, in what we have become. This is as it should be, for we are living beings that grow and develop and mature and evolve; we were never meant to be static. As the world unfolds before us, we in turn unfold before it—always testing, always trying something different, always searching for something new.

What is it that we really want? What will finally satisfy us? Will we in fact ever be fulfilled?

What we want is to understand this world in which we live, so that we can live in this world in which we are. What we really want is life—a life of peace and tranquillity, a life of challenge and excitement. We want to be daring but we want to be safe. We want to belong but we want to be free. We want to be mature but we want to stay young. We want to be like God! We want somehow to break loose from whatever confines us to time or to space or to habit or to limitation or to creaturehood. We want to transcend what we already have and are, in order to explore new possibilities, thrill to new experiences, learn from new insights. We want to be like God! We want to know and be known, to love and be loved. We want to mold and fashion and create, to discover and invent, to share what we have and what we are with others. We want to be like God! Sometimes we overstep our limits and try to *be* God, but we can only fail in the attempt. However, there is in the depths of our being a yearning that has never been assuaged. As enthralled as we are with the wonders of the universe, these cannot fulfill the longing within us. We want something more. We want to be like God!

As part of this world, a world that quickens us and refreshes us and piques our curiosity, we long for something beyond the world. Or perhaps one should say, we long for something beyond our perception of the world. We must experience and revel in our world, for it is beautiful and worthy of our acclaim, but it is not enough. Our hearts are restless and they will find peace only in God. And yet, as long as we have life, it is only in this world that we can find God or traces of God. While it may be true that at the heart of human striving is the ultimate search for God, this search occurs as we peer into the mysteries of creation. The sense of uneasiness and dissatisfaction that often overtakes us in the midst of success can bring us to the dawn of a new awareness, a realization that we can never be completely satisfied with what we have accomplished and in what we have become. It is foolhardy to glut ourselves with pleasures of any kind. Only God can fill us, and the only satisfying undertaking this life offers is the search for God in the midst of all human striving. This search, be it explicit or implicit, is the motivating force behind projects that serve to enhance human dignity, cherish human values, safeguard human well-being, and foster human development. Such projects elicit the noblest responses from women and men. When this happens we cannot be far from the fulfilling experience of God.

HAPPINESS

If we distrust our human nature we will be suspicious of anything that gives us pleasure or makes us happy. And yet, the refreshment that accompanies the taste of sweet cool water, the coziness we feel before a blazing fire, or the sense of invigoration that comes over us as we strain our muscles in energetic exercise, all issue quite naturally from our corporeal nature. The pleasure that we experience is frequently an inherent result of particular behavior. It is nature's way of telling us what we need in order to survive and to prosper.

But we are more than bodies, and by itself pleasure does not suffice. We seek a deeper fulfillment, a more satisfying enrichment. We know that only things "of the spirit" can make us happy. Thus we yearn for a sense of acceptance, of belonging; we want to participate in and share with; we are eager to learn. Happiness may well be more than a sunny sky on the day our team plays the championship game, or more than peanut butter not sticking to the roofs of our mouths. Yet happiness certainly is that quality of life we experience when we feel we can embark on our plans without being hampered by insurmountable obstacles, or when we are not frustrated in our endeavors. Happiness issues from a sense of fulfillment, a sense of accomplishment.

We play a significant role in deciding whether or not, and in what ways, we will be happy. We do this by selecting the values we will espouse, choosing the goals we will pursue, and setting the directions we will take. Happiness will be possible if the values are worthy of us, if the goals are realistic, and if the directions are accurate. True, all is not totally in our hands, but to a great extent we are responsible for our own happiness.

We cannot describe happiness because it comes under so many guises and effects us in so many ways, but we certainly know when we are happy. We smile to ourselves or we laugh out loud; sometimes we may even cry. We may babble or we may be speechless; we may jump up and down or we may sit in rapt silence. In spite of such diverse manifestations, every form of happiness includes a sense of well-being and the realization that it is good to be alive. This in turn can lead us to the God who has made us in such a way that we are able to rejoice. We were meant to be happy, and throughout life we search for what will bring it about. In so many ways we do find happiness, and yet there remains within us that deep unfulfilled yearning that can be satisfied only by God. We will know true happiness to the extent that we touch the mystery of God in life.

SUCCESS

What constitutes success? Wealth? Prestige? Victory? Does success consist in what we think of ourselves or in what others think of us? Is it the same as reputation? Is it to be understood in terms of what we have? Or what we do? Or what we are? Is it so wrong to want to be a success? Don't we have a right to rejoice in our accomplishments? It is because we are such complex beings that these questions do not allow for simple answers. It is because we are living human beings that grow and groan and strive and stretch that we reach out to what we have not yet attained, desirous of achieving our goal. Development, advancement, improvement are all inherent in the human condition. It is natural for us to want to succeed.

The question is: at *what* do we want to succeed?

Who of us does not want to have everything? Everything that is worthwhile. Everything that is honorable. Everything that is beneficial. Everything that has come from God. We were made to be filled with God and yet this fulfillment is presently beyond our reach. In this life we can attain God only through the things of God, and so we want them—all of them.

Who of us can live without the acceptance and affirmation of others? It is because we have been cherished by them that we can learn to esteem ourselves. Their opinion of our behavior helps us to determine its appropriateness. Their opinion of our accomplishment helps us to judge its quality. We are dependent creatures, dependent upon God but dependent upon each other as well. We will never really outgrow our need for approval.

Who of us can live with a constant overpowering sense of defeat? How many times can we be beaten down and still muster the strength and determination to try again? With all of its tenacity and resilience, the human spirit is nonetheless fragile. We must be able to cling to some bit of hope that what threatens our very existence will be overcome and that in the end we will prevail.

And so, what constitutes success? Wealth? Prestige? Victory? It must certainly be something other than the attainment of these goals, for they are out of the reach of so many of us. And yet reaching out for them, struggling to achieve them is possible for all of us. We can so easily lose our possessions, our reputation, or our footing, but we will not thereby forfeit the personal strengths and qualities that were developed as we applied ourselves to the tasks before us. Success lies in having developed the ability to manage and utilize the goods of this earth, in having been refined and enriched by the opinions of others, in having refused to allow our spirit to be ground underfoot. Success should be understood in terms of what we have become as human beings, as women and men of principle, women and men of faith.

SECURITY

Oh, to recapture the carefree days of childhood! To be able to run without apprehension or doubt! Oh, to feel secure once again! Why has the world become our enemy and life turned against us? Has growing up been detrimental to our safety? Or, have we always lived in danger, danger from which we were previously protected? Has security always been tenuous at best? Is vulnerability an inescapable consequence of our contingent transient existence?

We work so hard to protect ourselves from the weather, from our neighbors, from people we have never met and probably never will meet. We are afraid that we are going to lose our hold on life, that things are going to get out of hand. This is not groundless fear. It could very well happen. And so we band together. We join forces and talents, minds and hearts, and work interdependently to secure a foothold wherever possible. *With* each other, we do what we can to make the world safe *for* each other.

Only when we are secure can we hope to make any kind of progress. Only when we are secure do we have the leisure to stand in awe of the marvels of the universe. Only when we are secure can we live in peace with each other. We will only be secure if we place our trust in the right things and in the right people.

Economic security is so precarious! We can lose our life savings in a single business venture, in the wake of a natural disaster, or in a medical emergency. To put our trust in money is to build on sand. Even more distressing, nations compete rather than cooperate; they stockpile rather than share and all in the name of national security. We put our trust in sturdy horses, massive amphibians, and supersonic birds. Our confidence rests in our show of force. Finally, introspection has revealed a certain amount of fragmentation. Consequently, we endeavor to discover "our real selves," to "name" our strengths and weaknesses, and to "own" them. We hope thereby to gain a degree of personal security. But even integrated personalities are no guarantee of safe passage through a seemingly hostile world.

There is only one way to acquire and preserve a realistic sense of security. That is to live in harmony with the world of which we are a part, to acknowledge our mutual interdependence, and to foster cooperation wherever possible. Most assuredly, we should take pleasure in material things, protect ourselves from harm, and work toward the enrichment of our personalities. All the same, because we are creatures, the mutability and uncertainty of life cannot be avoided. Our only lasting security can be found in God. Clinging to God alone, we will be able to put all other securities in proper perspective.

IT FOLLOWS THAT, human aspirations, goals and pursuits originate in the desire to discover creation and the creator, and to live rewarding lives in the midst of this search and in the satisfaction of this discovery. Because we are limited and fallible, we make mistakes, sometimes serious mistakes. But we should not thereby hold ambition in contempt. We must be circumspect, but circumspection is not rejection. We should be emendatory, but emendation is not eradication.

God has endowed us with an inquisitive nature, with a spirit of adventure, and with a thirst for accomplishment. We must nurture our gifts not repress them. We must enhance our abilities not thwart them. We must direct our energies not stifle them. Reaching for more or for the most, desiring what is better or what is best, is indicative of the finite straining for the infinite, of a creature yearning for the creator. Such ambition is a requisite for prayer.

Humankind—Fearfully, Wonderfully Made

What is humankind that you are
mindful of it; weak human nature
that you care for it? You have made
it little less than divine, and
crowned it with glory and honor.

Psalm 8:4-5

In prayer we stand before God, eager to give and open to receive. We are not content merely to be creatures. We long to enter into a relationship with this ineffable mystery that persistently and patiently draws us ever more deeply into itself. The material traces of divine creativity that excite and delight us beckon us to a secret yet accessible meeting place. There we are intoxicated with a sense of God that permeates every dimension of our being and inundates our senses, our imaginations, our minds and hearts. We become the trysting place of the all-holy God and the world. It is in us and through us that creation is embraced by and embraces the creator in conscious loving communion. The more we enhance and refine the unique characteristics of our human nature, the better disposed we are for this union. Every faculty that we possess can serve to foster our involvement with the world of which we are a part and, thereby, provide us with access to this experience of God. Our prayer takes place in the world, with the world, and by means of the world. The world is truly a prayerful place.

INVOLVEMENTS

I ESTABLISH MY COVENANT

"Behold, I establish my covenant with
you and your descendants after you,
and with every living creature that is
with you, the birds, the cattle, and
every beast of the earth with you, as
many as came out of the ark. I establish my covenant with you, that never
again shall all flesh be cut off by
the waters of a flood, and never again
shall there be a flood to destroy the
earth."

Genesis 9:9-11

No one is an island. Try as we may, we cannot make it
alone. We need other things, other people; we need God. How
we see ourselves in relation to them will greatly influence how
we interact with them. If they seem to threaten us, we will assume a defensive stand and develop defensive attitudes. If they
seem to be inconsequential, we will be indifferent toward them
and dismiss them as irrelevant. If we view them as precious,

even friendly, we will stand open before them, willing to appreciate them or to offer and receive in mutual exchange.

Once again the Book of Genesis suggests a way of looking at life. Without denying the tensions that are part of human existence, the author provides us with a model for understanding the nature and quality of our fundamental relationships. This model is a form of covenant.

According to the narrative, Noah and his family are the only survivors of the flood. Representing the entire human race, they are called into covenant with God. Not only this particular generation but every succeeding generation will participate in this pact. Not only humans but every living thing on earth, even the earth itself, will be secure because of this covenant.

A covenant relationship presumes certain attitudes: attitudes of mutual cooperation and collaboration rather than unfair competition or arbitrary control; attitudes of genuine interdependence rather than restrictive dependence or disinterested independence; attitudes of unaffected respect and mutuality rather than unequivocal dominance or unqualified submission. As individual as we may be, we are, nonetheless, members of a universal community. God, the entire race, and all of creation are partners in this covenant. As a partner, God promises to preserve all living things, indeed, the earth itself. For its part, creation proceeds according to the laws of nature, thereby sustaining a certain ecological harmony. It seems that it is only the descendants of Noah who must learn what fidelity to the covenant requires of them. Only they seem to undermine social order. Only they seem to jeopardize environmental balance. Only they seem to stray from their commitment to God.

The nature and quality of our relationships with God, with each other, with the rest of creation are intimately linked with our attitudes toward life, the source of life, and the various manifestations of life. These attitudes and relationships reveal what kind of women and men we are, what kind of world view we espouse, what kind of lives we live, what kind of prayer we pursue.

At Peace with the World

For you shall be in league with the
stones of the field, and the beast of
the field shall be at peace with you.

Job 5:23

There are forces at work in the natural world that govern us, that can control us, that might destroy us. Survival demands that we live in harmony with these forces. Technology means that we have harnessed some of them. We have learned to use them for the attainment of our goals. We have learned to direct their energies for the accomplishment of our ends. We have learned to subdue the earth.

Though in many ways we may be like other living creatures, we have discovered how to use them to our advantage. We hunt them for food and for sport. We kill them in self-defence and for clothing. We domesticate them for work-power, for entertainment, and for companionship. We exercise dominion over the other creatures.

It appears that the evolutionary process moved from a state of the merely material to a point where life was vibrantly present in matter. Another quantum leap resulted in a form of conscious life. Human existence unfolds on this level. Ours is not merely material existence; nor is it only the experience of life. To be human is to be conscious, to think, to decide, to dream.

One would conclude that with these higher abilities we were meant to plumb the mysteries of the universe, to harness the power of nature, to rule over the creatures less developed than we. We have not only the desire but also the ability to do so. If, as evolution seems to indicate, we are the crown of creation, then surely creation should serve us in our striving for human comforts, human accomplishments, human perfection.

But nature does not only serve our physical needs, it serves our religious needs as well. Our liturgy is filled with the sounds and smells of the world; all used to help us to pray. Retreats are built in settings of spectacular beauty; all used to help us to pray. Lighting, form and design enhance our places of worship; all used to help us to pray. Our biblical tradition does speak of subjugation and dominion (Gen 1:26; 28), and thus belief in human superiority has strong religious grounding. Surely we are meant to bring the world into subjection and then offer it on high to the glory of God.

STILL . . . As we exercise the wondrous powers that are ours as human beings, we do not stand outside of our environment. It is, indeed, *our* environment. We breathe *in* it; we breathe *it*. Perhaps it is more correct to say that it breathes in us, for the world flows through us as food and breath and blood. Although we may discover and manipulate the laws of nature, we are still subject to them. We may be able to direct them, but we are not able to alter them. We have moved beyond the stage where we are at the mercy of nature. Now it appears that nature is frequently at the mercy of us. So it appears, but the appearance is deceiving. It is our environment, not nature, that is vulnerable before our technological achievements. Our technology, like everything in creation, is subject to the same physical laws. If we are to live and grow, to be conscious, to think and decide and dream, we must learn what our covenant with God and with the earth requires of us.

TO LIVE IN ACCORD WITH

We are so accustomed to using the things of the earth for our own purposes that we may fail to think of just exactly what we are doing to the earth as we use it. Nature itself has devised a mysterious and delicate balance whereby it continually renews itself. Death in one form gives way to life in a new form. Both animate and inanimate creation are governed by patterns of development that have brought forth the wondrous world of nature as we know it. These dynamic patterns regularly refashion the earth. However, if we intrude into the workings of nature without replacing what we have taken, or leave behind only the debris of our manipulation, we throw the entire environmental balance into jeopardy.

We are in covenant with the earth, in intimate and responsible relation to it. We are part of this mysterious and delicate balance. It takes place around us. It takes place within us. We are not disinterested bystanders but participants in the workings of nature. We did not weave the web of life; we are a strand in it. We are not above or separate from the natural world; in a very real sense we are a unique dimension of the world. We are not only warmed by the sun and nourished by the earth, we are captivated by nature. How else do we explain the awe that we experience looking at a starfilled sky, or the calm we feel walking through the woods? Or why do we become attached to animals? Is it not because we have a deep and abiding affinity with the rest of creation? We are a part of this mysterious network.

Everything we know we have learned from this world. True, we have powers to control it. We can consciously change some of the inner structure of its reality. We have learned much about genetic coding and we have made advances in genetic engineering. We can rearrange, but the same rules are operative. We can redirect cosmic radiation, alter topography, introduce new elements into the food chain, but the same rules are operative. We can assume the direction or redirection of these dynamic processes, but the same rules are operative.

What does it mean to "subdue the earth" and "have dominion over everything that moves upon the earth" if not to control them? Should not creation serve us in our striving for human comforts, human accomplishments, human perfection? Or must we deny our superiority in order to be in covenant with the earth?

The biblical narrative says that as earth-creatures we inhabit this earth along with the fish of the seas and birds of the air and every living thing that moves upon the earth (Gen 1:26, 28). But we, and only we, are images of God, which means primarily that we alone are signs of the sovereignty of God. As images we represent how and where *God* reigns supreme. As images we have the responsibility of fulfilling the role that *God* would fulfill. As images we must subdue and have dominion in the way that *God* would subdue and have dominion. Of all of the creatures of the universe, only we stand as unique signs and instruments of God's reign. The question of our superiority over other creatures is really a question of the manner of God's reign through us.

It would seem that God's will for the world is that it "be fruitful and multiply and fill the waters of the seas . . . and the earth" (Gen 1:22). It would seem that our responsibility as God's images and partners in the covenant is to see that this is accomplished. Since the earth itself appears to possess an inner urgency that strains toward this goal, we don't have to induce it. What we must do is safeguard it. As we test and probe and experiment, as we alter and redirect and fashion, as we subdue and have dominion, we must cherish the earth, nurture its fruitfulness and foster its growth. We can, indeed we must, exercise control over the earth, but this must be in accord with the processes that are operative within its very heart and within us as well.

These processes are far more than static laws. They are the dynamics of the entire universe. They are responsible for the course of the heavens, the shape of the earth, the complexity of life forms, the phenomenon of consciousness. There is a mysterious energy that has continually pressed forward. It is in the impulse of life and it is felt today in our strivings for progress and improvement, strivings that are breathtaking and noble but that must be kept in balance with the needs of the rest of the earth.

We alone of all the creatures of the earth can take hold of the powers of creation and reshape them for our own advancement. We alone have discovered fire and harnessed the energies of water, the wind, the sun, and the atom. We alone have the future of the earth's well being and survival in our hands. Possessing such power, we must never forget our covenant responsibilities. We must cherish the earth, nurture its fruitfulness and foster its growth. We must live in accord with our world or we will not live at all. We must be faithful to this covenant, a covenant not of our making but of God's. As images of God, we must walk through our world with dignity and authority, with understanding and trustworthiness. The earth is now in our keeping, the same earth from which we were born. We must take up this responsiblity as agents of God. It is an awesome role that we play in the world. It makes us stand in wonder at the magnificence of this universe and at the honor with which God has clothed us, a magnificence and an honor that are mere shadows of the glory of God.

TO BE SUSTAINED BY

As we ponder the mystery of life, our own life, one of the first questions we ask is: Why me? We did nothing to deserve life. But then the event of life is not an achievement. It is a pure gift which has been bestowed upon us. This is true of life itself, of the sustaining world into which we have been born, of the powers and abilities to unfold as individuals, to be enriched, and to assure the continuance of human life. Even the value and meaning of life is beyond our ability to determine. True, we do advance certain standards for "meaningful" living, but if they do not resonate with something that is innate, we quickly discard them for others more consistent with our nature. We are dependent upon our ancestors for our life, but even they received it as a gift. We are dependent upon our world for sustenance, but it too is but a thread in the vast network of life. We are dependent upon our heritage for our values, but tradition is merely the deposit of the wisdom of past generations. As we ponder the mystery of life, our own life, we stand in wonder before the giver of life, that reality that we call God.

We are not alone in this world, nor is it really *our* world. We are a part of the world that is God's, a world with interconnections, interrelationships, interdependencies. We are in covenant with the earth, in intimate and responsible relation to it.

The natural world shows us that life lives at the cost of other lives. Living things feed off of other living things. Our own life is sustained by other living things of our environment, an environment that replenishes itself according to its own inner processes. But it is an environment knitted to other environments in an intricate lace of living beings. To appropriate for our exclusive and indiscriminate use the environments of all living things is to ignore our responsibilities as images of God, to disregard the interconnections, interrelationships, interdependencies of the earth, and to endanger our own place in the world. To test and probe and experiment, to alter and redirect and fashion, to subdue and exercise dominion does not excuse us from heeding the natural processes of our world. If we do not allow the world to regenerate itself, if we do not allow the various levels of life to ebb and flow into waves of vitality, we are not signs of the reign of God but are false idols of human supremacy. We cannot arrogantly possess the earth. In fact, it will retaliate under human tyranny. Toxic streams already cause birth defects and nuclear radiation results in many forms of cancer. To subdue the earth and exercise dominion requires that we respect the complexity of our natural surroundings, surroundings that are the habitat of other kinds of living things.

How does this vibrant earth sustain us? It feeds us from its own substance as does a mother. In a very real sense it invites us, "Eat of my body, drink of my blood." Thus we become one with it, and it becomes a part of us. As we consume the earth, we need not diminish it. In the right measure, this can be a pruning which enables the earth to push forward with new life, new fruit. The earth sets a banquet before us. Its table is laden with roots that are fresh and sharp, with leaves that are tender and sweet. There are herbs and seeds and nuts, crispy grains whose mellow tones reflect the colors of the earth itself, fruits and berries that offer juices to satisfy every taste. There are meats and fish, there is milk and honey, and there is cool, clean, refreshing water. The earth reaches deep within itself and nourishes us from its very being.

It nourishes not only our bodies but our spirits as well. The shapes and contours, the brilliant and the muted tones, the textures and sublties of the natural world invade our senses. We are intoxicated by the aromas of early rain or freshly cut grass. The songs of morning birds, the wind in the trees, the crickets at night act as background melody for our daily lives. The earth makes artists, poets, mystics of each of us.

Just as every one of us has been given the mysterious gift of life, so every one of us can rely upon the earth to sustain that gift. Although life comes through other people, it is not really bestowed by those people. Nor is the earth and its sustenance given to us by others. All of this comes from God, the prodigious prodigal God. The earth must be maintained, it must be cultivated, but it cannot be exclusively possessed. It may be in the holding and within the stewardship of specific individuals or groups, but such land claims may never deprive others of what they need in order to survive and to flourish. The earth has been given to *us*, not to *me* or to *you* but to *us*, and we must share this earth with each other. We are equal partners in our covenant. Our relationship with the earth is a communal relationship. Noah represented all of the people who were saved from destruction. This included future generations as well. "Behold, I establish my covenant with you and your descendants after you" (Gen 9:9).

The earth unsparingly offers us food and drink with a liberality like that of God. No questions are asked; no one is turned away. Having been born into life is reason enough to be sustained. This realization can bring us to our knees in humble gratitude. But we cannot stay there. As images of God, we must safeguard the fruitfulness of the earth and we must share the earth with all of creation, but most especially with each other. The liberality of God will then radiate from the images of God, which we are.

TO CARE FOR

The wonder, the gratitude and the liberality that well up within us as we behold the world and realize our participation within it spill over into compassionate and reverent care for it. We can direct its energies for the accomplishment of our ends while at the same time cherishing the earth, nurturing its fruitfulness and fostering its growth. We can do this by assuming our mission as images of God and trustworthy caretakers of the earth.

The earth is a storehouse of mineral and fossil treasure.

Having discovered it, we have become captivated with its power. The child in us seeks to find out more and more, to push it further and further. The responsible steward in us must secure the outer limits of our searching and our testing lest we squander our treasure and it be lost to us forever. This treasure may well be used for our development, but not for our exploitation.

The earth vibrates with the pulsations of life, works miracles of renewal within the secrets of its body, and then feeds us with the outward signs of these miracles. Our insatiable appetites want more and more and better and better. As responsible stewards we must be considerate about the strains that maturation can bear and patient with its timing. The fruits of the earth are for our nourishment, but not for our hoarding.

Our beautiful earth has been gorged and ravaged, polluted and stripped, and all the while it willingly offered its wealth asking only that it be taken with care and planning. We did not know we were to be responsible stewards rather than indulged children. This is one of the lessons that the earth is teaching us now. We will discover what stewardship means. We will learn to reclaim the land, purify the water, freshen the air. The fish and birds and everything that moves upon the earth will "increase and multiply and fill the waters of the seas . . . and the earth." We will learn this, or we will not survive.

Our generous earth has been captured and possessed by some to the exclusion of others. We have claimed its riches as our own, while our sisters and brothers languish in poverty. We have sated ourselves with its produce, while others starve at our feet. We have amassed and we have stored what we will never be able to use, while others wither away in desperation. We have not yet learned to be stewards of God's earth. What we have, we have in trust, to be distributed where there is need. The warmth, the comfort, the refreshment of the earth belongs to everyone. As images of God, we merely manage it in God's name. We will discover what stewardship means. We will feed the hungry, give drink to the thirsty, clothe the naked. Without denying the human need to be somehow identified with a specific piece of land and the rights that accompany this need, we will learn better to distribute the wealth of the earth or we will not survive as a society.

ON THESE GROUNDS, let us turn to the origins of our existence; to the earth from which we were born; to the sun, the real source of our life; to the stars from which it all began. Let us turn with gratefulness, with respect, and with awe. The earth has been patient and gentle and unselfish as it provides us with food and clothing and shelter and beauty. The sun has warmed us, given us light, and taught us to tell time. And the stars have never ceased to draw us out of ourselves, beyond the confines of our world into the vastness of space. In the face of all of this magnificence, *we* are called images of God.

We are only beginning to realize that being the image of God is a distinction that brings with it serious responsibilities. We are signs of the sovereignty of God; we represent how and where God reigns supreme. In humble recognition of this, we will not attempt to control the earth, but will live in accord with it; we will not claim possession of the earth, but will be grateful to be sustained by it; we will not exploit the earth, and others through the earth, but will care for it and share its riches. As we do this, we manifest the tender compassion that our God has toward all creation.

Living in covenant with the earth will give us freedom. We will be able to follow it as it draws us into the secrets of its heart, there to find God. We will be sensitive to its twists and to its turns, to its cries and to its silences, and know God's presence through it all. We will learn what it has to teach us of the creative amusement of God, of the youthful imagination of God, of the profound wisdom of God. Here we will look on the face of God and live.

You will be My People

Behold, I am toward God as you are;
I too was formed from a piece of clay.
Behold, no fear of me need terrify you;
My pressure will not be heavy upon you.

Job 33:6-7

The human heart has known both an attraction and an aversion toward other people. They are fascinating and threatening; they entertain and they seduce us; they yield to us and they dominate us. In our search for fulfillment, for perfection, we are attentive to others as inspirations and guides along the path to God, and we take flight from them as temptations or obstacles on the way.

Spiritual teachers have insisted that we must love God with an undivided heart. We must only love others *in* God and *God* in them. We have been made for God alone; we are restless until we rest in God. In our struggle to understand what this means, we have undertaken exercises of discipline aimed at stripping us of worldly attachments. We have established schools of devotion that seek to lift us to a supernatural realm.

We have devised systems of religious thought designed to concentrate our attention on the things of God. And all of this for the benefit of the individual.

Frequently life has been depicted as the personal journey of the soul. We will definitely meet others on the way and they may even journey with us for a while, but ultimately it is our own journey and our own way. We can learn from them and be enriched by their wisdom, but it will then be our own learning and enrichment, contributing to our own fulfillment.

Every person is unique and must discover the dimensions of this uniqueness. Each soul is like a delicate instrument that will tremble with its own specific quality. Only God knows the melody of which it is capable; only God can perceive the patterns of its composition. True, it can make its unique contribution to the total human symphony, a contribution that only it can make, yet the ensemble can perform without it. Furthermore, a well-crafted instrument can draw music from its own genius in solo fashion. Ultimately, it is one of a kind.

BE THAT AS IT MAY...No one is an island. No one is really independent of others. We are all interdependent, not merely because of need and desire, but because of origin and destiny, because of nature. Being human cuts across distinctions of gender, age, race, class or national allegiance. We cannot afford to be separated from others. If we look upon them merely as "other," we risk measuring their value only in terms of their usefulness to us. How fascinating are they? How entertaining? How yielding? Do they inspire us? Do they guide us? Do they bring us to God? On the other hand, if we look upon others as original expressions of the imagination of

God, they are then seen as counterpoints in the divine polyphonic composition. They may well be "other," but only as night is other to day, as spring is other to fall, as ebb is other to flow.

The natural world has shown us that the greater the differentiation, the greater the perfection of the whole. It is in the intricate interaction of diversity that the beauty of the world unfolds. It is in the intricate interaction of incomparable individuals that the magnificence of the creator is manifested. The "other" participates, as we participate, in the adventure of life.

THE OTHER PERSON

Male and female God made them. Both are created in the image of God. Both are commissioned to increase and multiply and fill the earth. Both have the responsibility of subduing and of having dominion. Neither one is better; neither one preferred. God looked upon the two of them, together, and saw that it was good. Together they would carry the mystery of life forward. Together they would discover the world with all its secrets. Together they would gather creation within their very beings and bring it to God in thanksgiving.

Through the ages women and men have always been a mystery to each other, wondering how we are alike, and how we are different. At various times in various ways we have defined, circumscribed, and restricted ourselves and each other. We are only beginning to realize how limiting this has been.

Men and women are meant to be partners, not rivals. As partners we fashion the first and most basic union of minds and hearts and bodies, that union from which is born new life. As partners we mold this new life and open it to the wonders of the world. As partners we strengthen each other; we inspire each other; we support each other. As partners we share wisdom and feeling and humor.

This partnership is both sustaining and surprising. We do not know which one will be stronger or which one will have more insight. We are not sure if one is intuitive, if one is indecisive, or who is leader. The unfolding of the other will be as unpredictable as will be the discovery of oneself.

This partnership is not so much one of equality as one of mutuality and harmony, for no two people have the same abilities and limitations; no two people have the same qualities of mind and heart. No two people are alike. Discovering the uniqueness of each other as persons, we then create a relationship never again to be duplicated, an energetic relationship that shatters all stereotypes.

We do not so much complement each other as draw out the latent riches of the other. Our gender does not determine the many facets of personality. That is determined by our uniqueness, a uniqueness bestowed by God and then called forth by love and tenderness. In this relationship with the other, we mold and fashion; we bring to birth and we nurture the delicate life we cherish. In this relationship with the other, we enter into the creative activity of God.

THE OTHER TIME

What is the "flower of youth?" How long does it bloom? Does it always wither and die, or can it be renewed with the dew of each dawn? And how many years must timber endure before it is considered "seasoned"? Does time really make everything better? Is there a natural antagonism between what was and what is coming to be, or is it we who have pitted them against each other? Is it not possible, indeed, necessary, for the past and the future to embrace in the present?

Although ours is a society constantly on the lookout for the new, the different, the unusual, we must learn to show great reverence for our elderly. They are not like old newspapers to be stacked, or old clothes to be boxed, or old ideas to be stored in archives. They are the living records of our heritage. They have weathered the changes of the world, and they have endured. They have seen the rise and fall of empires, and they have remained. They are the bridges joining the past with the present. In their time, they preserved what they thought was the best of their inheritance, enriched it, imaginatively reinterpreted and transformed it, and then openhandedly presented it to us in the hope that it would enhance our lives.

On the other hand, if our attraction to youth is more than a superficial infatuation with external form and style, we must be attentive to youth's endearing yet fragile qualities, its as yet unmanaged new physical and psychic strength. We must be diligent in our caring for them lest they disappear before they can be transformed into something that can endure. Make-believe and pretend are the stuff of hopes and dreams. Magic and mystery are fuel for the imagination. And innocence and trust must never be shattered but must mature and become astute.

Both old age and youth are times of such vulnerability. Steps are unsure; the world seems strange and hostile. We are either no longer or not yet capable, no longer or not yet useful. And still, what possibilities each holds; and together, what a combination of creative energies. Hand in hand the learning of the past and the dreams of the future can collaborate in creative explorations of the mind. Hand in hand the stability of the past and the adventure of the future can forge the way towards new horizons of possibility. Hand in hand the wisdom of the past and the questioning of the future can meet in continuing search for the deeper meaning of life.

No time of life is indispensible; or period is trivial. What is human is always worthy of our attention and of our respect. The elderly need the young in order to keep company with the soul of their own youth. And the young have need of the assurance of those who know well the seasons of life. And through it all, the moments of life converge in the timelessness of God.

THE OTHER COLOR

The configurations and shadings of the earth have appeared in the faces of its people. Following the contours of the land, they are smooth and rounded, or drawn and stark, or broad and craggy, or finely chiseled. The colors are like the lush dark humus of the rain forest, the sun-baked adobe of the mesa, the fertile alluvial silt of the river bed, the olive tone of powdery clay, and soft tinted sand of the prairie. The countless variations of form and feature and hue mirror the kaleidoscopic inventiveness of life.

Even the climate elicits various characteristics of the human personality. The hot steaming tropics seem to hypnotize with its spell, moving the serene and unhurried people to and fro in gentle movement. The winds and rain have cut deeply into other spirits, leaving them as weathered and sculptured and as strikingly awesome as the surrounding canyons. Rich fertile land, that is prodigal in providing those fruits of the earth that both delight and nourish, asks little of the harvester but a light heart and a grateful spirit. There is a stability and permanence to the clay of the river banks that does not deny its translucent character. Many years of refinement at the seasonal wheel and kiln of hardship have brought forth in some people the delicacy of porcelain. The plains and grasslands have given birth to as many kinds of people as it has produced grains, tender and sweet, sturdy and enduring, and as constant as the earth itself.

Every kind of land, every kind of climate, has raised up women and men who are in tune with its rhythms and attentive to its moods. Reaching deep within the common store of human possibility, these people have discovered what they need to survive and to flourish wherever they find themselves, and they have adapted to the versatility of the earth in remarkable ways.

It is the earth and its environments that are responsible for some of our differences, differences that are proof of ingenuity, not of superior or inferior quality. One cannot rank the earth's surfaces by color or physical characteristics, deciding which is more beautiful or which is more necessary. Neither can one rank the earth's people. Our colorings and our physical characteristics are the complexion and the profile of the entire human community. And the eye does not say to the ear, "I have no need of you." Together we form a human mosaic with various textures and composition, evidence of the artistry of the creator.

THE OTHER LIFE

We all have the same basic necessities, but we do not all have access to the goods that will meet our needs. Those who have influence control the goods; and the poor we have always with us. We all have unique talents, but some are more adept at producing and managing than are others; and the workers we have always with us. We all have intelligence and insight, but some are exceptional in their mental abilities and acquire funds of knowledge; and the simple folk we have always with us. Those with influence and ability and information wield the power. It is power that classifies us in our contemporary western world. There are the powerful and the powerless; the haves and the have-nots; those in and those out. But power is merely the ability to do or to accomplish something. The pressing question is, "How is power exercised?"

It can be exploitative, robbing people of whatever they have. The poor become the property of the rich, losing not only the little they hold but even their own self-possession. The energies of the workers become the fuel for the insatiable machinery of progress. The simple folk are tricked into unquestioning allegiance.

Power can be manipulative, using people for its own ends. Having little or nothing, the poor become dependent upon the very ones who use them. The workers have little to say about their manner of work or the conditions in which they perform their tasks. The simple folk are indoctrinated with the prevailing philosophy.

And power can be competitive, pitting one class against the other. The poor are treated as potential insurrectionists who must be restrained. Workers too have to be held in check lest they strike and shut down production. New ideas are the seeds of revolution and should be kept far from the simple folk.

But power can also be nutritive, enriching the lives within its circle of influence. It can be the voice of advocacy for the poor who are not otherwise heard. It can be an enabling force pledged to providing more and more opportunity for the collaboration of the workers. It can be the inspiration that challenges the simple folk to seek new avenues of self-determination.

And it can be integrative, enveloping all in a mutual embrace of solidarity. The poor can reclaim their rightful place in society as integral members worthy of respect. Workers can resume their responsibilities as partners in the common task of stewardship of the earth. Simple folk can entertain their own perspective on life free of intimidation. Those with influence and ability and information can share the power.

In the biblical tradition, God is portrayed as a God of righteousness, concerned for the well-being of all, and taking steps to ensure that nothing stands in the way of its accomplishment. In our efforts to be one with this God, we cannot be blind to the needs of others nor deaf to their cries. The righteousness of God will only touch their lives as we touch their lives. It is through us that they will know that God is a living God, compassionate and overflowing with loving-kindness.

THE OTHER LAND

Who has not known a tightening of the throat at times of great national pride? When the noble ideals upon which the country has been founded are expressed in the lives and the deaths of its sons and daughters, national honor and national loyalty permeate our consciousness.

There is a certain elusive quality that marks one people off from another. It is a kind of second nature, an unwritten law that all learn to observe. It can be heard in the speech patterns of the people, in their choice of words and images. It flows silently through their way of life, the beliefs they hold, the customs they follow. It reveals itself in their dress, their music, their art. This elusive quality is the national spirit.

Group identity developed out of a basic human need to work together for survival and well-being. It seems to be inexorably linked to land, because the people must be materially sustained as they are politically organized. The character of the supply of natural resources and wildlife determine whether a people will be settled or migratory, thriving or destitute. The primary responsibilities of the leadership are to manage the material wealth of the land and to protect it from invasion. Nations enjoy a certain amount of territorial sovereignty.

While the flame of patriotism is often fed by a passionate attachment to the land that we have come to know and love, it is the values that it espouses and the way of life that it encourages that sustain the deep commitment we have for our nation. These values and this way of life must be honest expressions of the ideals that inspired the country's founding. In spite of its failures, our country must keep ever before its eyes the highest standards to which it has committed itself. But then the country is not some mammoth amorphous reality. *We* are the country. They are *our* ideals, *our* values, *our* standards. *We* are the ones who must keep them before our eyes.

Patriotism has inspired some of the most heroic behavior in human history. For its sake, people have put at risk reputation and position, possessions and security, even life itself. What makes it so ennobling is that it is a commitment to ideals and not merely to structures or to policies. It can be critical of leadership or of membership without being disloyal.

If we have a deep appreciation of the dynamics behind our own love of country, we will honor the devotion other people have for their lands. Chauvinism will find no place in our minds and hearts. It does not follow that when we hold to our values we should disdain what others cherish. Nor does commitment to national progress open the door to international imperialism. Such attitudes are the precursors of war, while mutual regard and cooperation are the guardians of peace. Every nation has its own strengths, its own character, its own dreams that express and foster human unfolding. Because they spring from the human heart, they are worthy of our respect. It is by standing with open mind before the unfamiliar that we learn to stand with open heart before the unknown God.

CONSEQUENTLY, joined with others by the threads of human existence, we need not sever them as we come before God in prayer. As we stand in conjunction with others, so we stand before God. What we learn in our relationships with them, we bring to our relationship with God.

We do not merely marvel at the creative powers of God, we take part in them. We join actively in fashioning women and men into sensitive, vital companions who are then part of us regardless of where we are. In addition to this, we open ourselves to be shaped by them, by their wisdom and fidelity, their patience and their trustworthiness. They have touched our spirits and their influence lives within us. Since we are mutually open and vulnerable before each other, it is not difficult to be open and vulnerable before God. When we stand thus, the gentle touch of God can create us anew.

For everything there is a season; everything has its proper time, and the secret of time is in the timeless God. If there is anything out of our control, it is time. We cannot rush it; we cannot hold it back. All we can do is accept it. Accepting it we can learn something of the inevitabilities that are beyond our control, indeed, beyond our comprehension. We can only live in the presence of these incomprehensibilities and trust. This too is a disposition that leads us into contemplation.

If "the world is charged with the grandeur of God" what shall we say of the people of the world? Each reflects divine originality, a slightly different shade, a distinctive form, a certain disposition. As we gaze in awe at the creation, we acknowledge with awe the creator.

If there is anything of God that the world needs at this time, it is compassion. Not merely a feeling of sympathy, but a burning desire to alleviate the cause of misery and pain. Let us learn this compassion by looking first into the eyes of suffering and then into the heart of God. We will not learn compassion if we go to God alone.

Our world has become too small for us to persist in any isolationist attitude. It is too easy to know about other people, other cultures. Information about people from all over the world is available at our fingertips. Much that was once unfamiliar can now be understood. How can we be disinterested, unreceptive or hostile toward others and still think that we can be attentive, docile, and reverent toward God? The way we live is the way we pray.

I Will be Your God

> Can you find the deep thing of God?
> Can you find out the limits of the
>   Almighty?
> It is higher than the heaven—
>   what can you do?
> Deeper than Sheol—what can you
>   know?
> Its measure is longer than the earth,
>   and broader than the sea.
>
> *Job 11:7-9*

We have all been taught about God and the deeds of God. We learned about this from our parents and from our teachers. We've marveled at the stories of how God led the people out of bondage and into a land bursting with life, of how God first sent prophets to warn and then conquerors to punish. We are sobered by the tales of war and destruction, but we are consoled by the promises and the announcement of the messiah. The history of the human race has been described as the history of sin and punishment.

We have pondered this sacred history, and within it the revelation of God that made it sacred, in order to sanctify our own times. We have interpreted the events of our days in light of this hallowed record and we have tried to chart the future accordingly. We have entered the accounts of our lives as a chapter in this ever-unfolding drama of salvation.

The God who is revealed through all of this is a God who

enters into history as a participant, as one who goes in front of the people in their journeys, as one who directs their destiny, as one who acts on their behalf. This God is seen as an intrepid trailblazer, a fierce warrior, a stern judge, a forgiving savior. It is a God who makes exacting demands of those who have been called.

It is very difficult to list our obligations in order of importance. However, one of the most significant is obedience. The divine laws that were revealed and that have been handed down to us today lay open the duties we have toward this God who has entered our history. Obedience is certainly one of our primary responsibilities.

Along with obedience we think of worship. We do not believe that God needs our devotion; it is we who need to be devout. We need to pay homage to that being who is obviously in control of everything; to express the gratitude in our hearts; to make amends for our failings; and to ask for what is essential for life. Worship springs from deep within us and we own it to God.

Probably the most exalted response to God is that of love. The prophets call for this as do the psalmists. We should love God as God has loved us. Our entire history shows us how God has loved us, has taken us from nothing and has formed us into a people, has protected us from harm and has saved us from utter destruction. In view of such marvelous deeds, we should turn to God in grateful love.

These are but a few of the sentiments that are stirred within us as we ponder the events of our sacred history.

ALL THE SAME . . . As thrilling as the thought is that God is an active participant in the historical unfolding of a particular people, there is another setting wherein God's purposes are discovered. This is the universal experience of life itself. It is there that all women and men must confront the fundamental questions of life and decide for or against honor, for or against integrity, for or against God.

As sacred as are the holy traditions of our faith, the narratives, the prophecies and the psalms, there are other lessons that we must learn about God. These lessons we cannot learn from others. They are lessons of wisdom, and of righteousness, and of mystery. They are the lessons of life. In order to learn them we must search for the truth, listening with all the diligence of which we are capable. We must enter wholeheartedly into the exploration of life, and there we will find God.

IN CREATION

Creation itself is a never-ending source of knowledge. As we learn more and more about the wonders of this world, we discover certain laws or patterns, laws or patterns that govern our life as well.

We so often take for granted the variety of life forms with which our earth is blessed. A moment spent in a garden where color and aroma invade the senses or in a woods clothed with radiant autumn foliage will quickly remind us of its lavish adornment. Animals too are so different. The same area can be home for two- and four-legged creatures, birds and insects as well as fish. Amidst such diversity, some mysterious balance seems to have been achieved in nature. The life force that pulses within one form is restrained by the life force within another, and everything contributes to the vitality of the whole. This harmony and interdependence is a marvel to behold. We know that certain laws or patterns are operative, but we are not sure *why* life, our life included, behaves as it does.

The non-living world too both teaches and raises questions. Some objects fall while others rise. We have discovered the principles of gravity, but are still puzzled as to why things are attracted to each other in the first place. We understand that some things are lighter than air, but we don't know why some atomic particles react in one way and others in another. If, indeed, energy darts back and forth out of and into existence, why does it act that way? Should we ever be able to explain why these things act or react as they do, we will still be faced with another question—is it really all only due to random selection or chance?

All of our experiments and probings and studies seem to lead us to the same question: what is the source of all of this regularity, this interdependence, this harmony, this balance? It is no wonder that our ancestors worshipped nature, not merely because of its beauty or because of its power, but because of its mystery. They frequently referred to this mystery as wisdom, and cried out in wonder, "Where shall wisdom be found? And where is the place of understanding?" Search as they may, search as *we* may, this wisdom is beyond the grasp of human comprehension. We stand dumfounded before the questions of nature, the questions from the whirlwind:

> How were the foundations of the earth laid?
> How were its measurements determined?

How are the seas kept in place?
Where does the animal get its instinct?
How did the horse get its strength?
What makes the hawk soar?

Whether we respond to the questions with myth or with science, the answer is the same—God! We may be able to chart the progress that the world has made, but we cannot thereby uncover its secret. It came from some numinous reality, it is sustained in mystery, and it seems to tend toward something we cannot perceive. We are governed by this same mystery, not merely by the laws of nature but by the mystery in which these laws are grounded. We have but to follow the example of the rest of creation and surrender ourselves to it. There is no need to fear, for it is this mystery that has brought us into being and continues to carry us tenderly next to its heart. It calls to us gently but constantly through the beauty and the challenge of the world, if we will only listen. Though this mystery, this wisdom, will always elude us, we will be able to follow its traces if we do not give up the search.

This wisdom that we seek in creation was set up before the beginning of the earth. It was present when God established the heavens, marked out the foundations of the earth, and set limits to the sea. It is God's wisdom, and that is why it is a mystery, and why it is inaccessible.

This presence of God, this stirring of God in the world, cannot be localized as can be the episodes in the story of salvation. It is too rudimentary, too elusive, and more like a constant dynamic than a historical event. Nor does it lend itself to human-like conceptions such as trailblazer, warrior, judge or savior. The language we use to speak of this divine manifestation may sound impersonal—creator, origin, source.

But what does one call the thriving, burning, intoxicating mystery within reality?

IN RIGHTEOUSNESS

As the imperceptible and inaccessible power of balance and harmony that sustains creation is called wisdom, so the relationship of balance and harmony within society is called righteousness. As with wisdom in creation, so righteousness within the community not only allows the individual to follow its own inner urgings, but it fosters its growth, its flowering and its full bloom. It does this while at the same time weighing the force of the individual against the vigor of each of the others within the group. Righteousness is an ineffable governing capacity like the genius of the conductor, that teases out the potential of each instrument, knowing when its tones should dominate and when they should support the melody; or like the artistry of the painter, who brushes brilliance next to sublety in such right proportion as to create a work of distinctive beauty.

As with wisdom, such righteousness is beyond our ability to comprehend, for we cannot sound the depths of the spirit wherein is found the real identity of the individual. We are ignorant of the dignity of which each is capable, of the warmth and devotion, of the love. Such righteousness belongs to God, who alone searches the hearts and knows the secret longings found there, who alone can weave the warp and woof of countless tones and textures into a fabric that features each at the expense of none. And this is true righteousness! It is the righteousness of God that knows the appropriate time and measure of each entrance, and that can subdue or silence without putting to death. And this is true justice!

It follows that it is the righteousness of God that cries out if one of us should be denied the opportunity to emerge or to advance. It is the righteousness of God that is spurned when our power and authority are not exercised peaceably or fairly. When God's righteousness is ignored it must be restored, not for God's sake, but for ours. It is not so much that God punishes as that we bear the weight for our decision for imbalance or disharmony.

Our attempts at justice are faint reflections of this righteousness. Our vitality as a people is dependent upon our ability to retain these fleeting but ever-recurring reflections. We cannot capture them once and for all, because righteousness is not a static reality like the laws and the statutes that are intended to guard it. It is supple and responsive to the tendencies and variations of changing human beings. We cannot fully comprehend it, nor can we force it to meet our narrow and unyielding standards of justice. But we long for it, and we search for it, and we try to live in accord with it, halting though our attempts may be. We know that it is only within this righteousness that we will know fulfillment and peace. For it knows what is for our welfare far better than we do, but it does not impose itself upon us. Like wisdom, it calls to us gently but constantly. It calls through the tension we feel between our own need to be seen and heard and the right that others have for the same expression; through the passion we experience seeing others dispossessed, neglected, or abandoned. These are the promptings of God's righteousness.

Being of God, righteousness is both within and beyond. It is the ground upon which each relationship stands. It is the standard against which all is judged. Yet it cannot be scrutinized. Being of God, it is constant and true, it is enlivening and discerning, it is merciful and compassionate. Divine righteousness is the tender caress of a God who knows and cares.

IN MYSTERY

Who can even begin to imagine the mystery that is God? We need no tradition to tell us that God is ineffable; we can come to that realization by ourselves. The numinous within creation, regulating and balancing, and the hidden stream of righteousness that flows beneath the surface of human community are not the only manifestations of the mystery that we call God. All we need do is ponder and consider.

What is it in life that we invariably turn toward as the leaf turns toward the sun? What is the compelling attraction that seems ever-present yet out of reach? What is it that dips into the center of our beings and draws us out into—into what? Into itself. It is the light that brings everything into focus, but cannot itself be seen. It is the silence that carries every sound. It is the God that we know about, until we come to know.

What is it toward which all of our yearnings tend? What is the final goal of our striving? Wherein do we find our peace? Our rest? Why have we . . . you and I . . . even been brought into this constant flow of becoming, and disclosure, and pressing forward? Why?—Because! We . . . you and I . . . have been called by, attracted to, and loved by, God. And why?—Because!

We strain forward toward that which is already within and within which we are. We search for what we already possess and what possesses us. We seek to fill ourselves with what can only empty us, to contain within ourselves that which is boundless. We are finite beings with an inclination toward the infinite. We yearn for God.

We are overwhelmed by the radiance of the universe, its symmetry, its power,—but it is not enough. We are speechless before human creations, music and art, structure and form, imagery and thought—but it is not enough. Behind all of this, within all of this, is something else, something that we know but we cannot comprehend. It is the reason why; it is the explanation of how. It is the place from which and to which; it is now. It is!

And so we continue to turn toward it, to be compelled by it, to search for it, because that is all we can do. We continue to ask questions, the answers of which we already know, because that is all we can do. We believe and trust, and believe further and trust more deeply, because that is all we can do. We immerse ourselves in the mystery in which we are already immersed, and we will know that this is God.

IN LIFE

If we cannot now behold the face of God but only the wake of God's passing, what good is life? Should we not long to be released from limitation and dissolved into the unknown? But this world, this life, is so much a part of us and we of it. It is truly bone of our bone and flesh of our flesh, and it is only within *it* that we touch and are touched by God. To be who we are, alive in this place and at this time, in relationship with these people is all that we need to experience God.

Our insatiable desire for insight and understanding comes not so much from an emptiness as from a taste of God that we have already savored. This taste has whetted our appetite for more and it will not be satisfied. Thus, as we savor again and again the sweetness of this truth, we realize that it is only in such pursuits that we will be nourished on God.

Our appreciation for what is beautiful is a doorway through which we step into a world of delicacy and charm as well as opulence and splendor. It is there that we are soothed by God's gentleness and awakened by God's appeal. We are attracted and we become attached. We are allured and we become captivated. We have been possessed by God and we surrender.

Where? All the world is a sacred precinct. All the world is holy ground. All the world is the place of encounter with God. God is not hidden in the mountains or the caves; God does not prefer the woods or the open plains, but walks the streets of the cities and the paths of the slums, through avenues and alleyways as well. We need not travel to another place; we need only be attuned to the place where we are. For if not here—where?

When? The revelation of God is neither a thing of the past nor reserved for some mystical moment in the future. Every moment is mystical for it provides us with the opportunity of an encounter with God. Now is the acceptable time. For if not now—when?

But most of all it is in our relationships with others that we experience God. This experience takes the numerous shapes of the events of our day. It is mirrored in the faces of those who make up our lives. We know it in the care we give to those in need, and in the favors that we receive from others. It comes to us softly and tenderly as the touch of love, or as unyielding and determined as is conviction. Committed to each other, we struggle through anger and pain lest misunderstanding or weakness drive a wedge between us and leave us both in isolation. It is God who sustains us in this struggle until together we can rest in peace.

The experience of human life is the setting wherein God's purposes are discovered. It is there that we learn the lessons of wisdom and of righteousness and of mystery. It is there that we encounter God.

ACCORDINGLY, we begin to understand God less specifically, but more deeply. This mysterious reality is not domesticated, trained to answer us when *we* call, but is all-pervasive, sustaining us, beckoning to us, encouraging us, welcoming us. We do not pray for God's presence in our midst but for an awakening to our presence in the midst of God. We do not pray for God's protection but for our abandonment to the embrace of God's concern. We need tell God nothing; we have but to listen and to learn.

We, who are so extraordinary and so wondrously made, are yet so circumscribed, so limited. We stand humbly, but not humbled, before and within the wisdom and the righteousness that is God, the God who holds all things together in order and in love. We stand silently, but not silenced, before and within the mystery that is God, the God who sweeps us out of ourselves into the incomprehensible. This is the God with whom we are in covenant, the God who has desired us from before the beginning.

How then does one pray? Better still—what, then, is not prayer?

All Things Work Together unto Good

For the whole creation in its nature
was fashioned anew,
complying with your commands,
that your children might be kept
unharmed.

Wisdom 19:6

In prayer we stand in covenant with God, with others, and with all of the world. We stand clothed in both privilege and in responsibility. We are images of God, living signs of God's undisputed reign. We have been crowned with honor and glory and we act as stewards over all of creation. We cannot help but be grateful to and compassionate toward our world. It has been faithful to us, feeding us and clothing us, giving us shelter and warmth, It is, indeed, a good earth!

As significant as is our privilege, we also carry the weight of its responsibility. We are signs of the reign of God, not false idols of human supremacy. The world has been placed in our keeping to till and to guard, not to exploit or to squander. We cannot live without this earth. We need it as it needs us. And so we bring this mutual dependence before the God upon whom everything relies. And we stand in humble need and total confidence.

From the very beginning, our fulness as people has been expressed as community; male and female we were created. We are not brought into being in isolation, nor even by only one other person. We are brought into being through a community, through a woman and a man. We carry within ourselves traces of our ancestors. We express ourselves in the manner of our own specific people. We are formed by those who love us and those who don't. No one is a stranger to us. All belong to God and there we are all one. The more united we are to others in mutual respect and cooperation, in understanding and in harmony, the more complete is the person we bring to prayer. For in each person God sees the entire race, and God views the whole race as though it were one person.

Creation, both our own and that of the world, seems to spring from a gratuitous act of God. The same can be said about the covenant. Perhaps it is more correct to say that God established the covenant by the act of creation itself. We do not deserve it, but being in covenant makes us deserving. Words cannot express this mystery; too many words have tried to. How should one respond to this? With praise? With gratitude? Can one even respond? This prayer is silence in God, and it occurs in the world, a prayerful place.

DESTINIES

MY LIFE IS IN YOUR HANDS

Let your tears fall for the dead,
and as one who is suffering
grievously, begin the lament.

Sirach 38:16a

My spirit is broken, my days are
extinct, the grave is ready for me.

Job 17:1

The greatest possession we have is life. Without it we have nothing else. As we consider its marvelous workings we come to see that it is really not a possession. It is a gift, something that we may have at our disposal for a time, but only for a time. We did nothing to attain it and, try as we may, we cannot cling to it forever.

Our biblical ancestors held this view. They believed that all life came from God and returned to God. What made human life so exceptional was the conviction that God had entered into a special relationship with the race and had chosen to lavish the blessings of divine love on those who would receive them. Real life was friendship with God and anything that threatened this friendship, or might diminish the ability to enjoy these blessings, was viewed as some form of death. With no clear conception of an afterlife where fulfillment would be possible, the ancients grasped earthly life with fervor and trembled with apprehension at the prospect of suffering and death.

It is the dearness of life that makes suffering and death so abhorrent. Only those who take no pleasure in life want to die. It is natural that we should cling even to the slightest hope of survival. And it is just that—hope. It is not an empty hope, but one grounded in our experience of the goodness of life and the compassion of God from whom all life comes.

Where Is God Now?

> Have pity on me, have pity on me,
> O you my friends,
> For the hand of God has touched
> me.
>
> Job 19:21

As soon as we declare that God is good and life is beautiful, we come up against the reality of suffering. How can a loving God allow it to happen? The biblical tradition and spiritual writers of all traditions have tried to answer this question. Sometimes the answers given in the various traditions are very similar; at other times they are quite distinctive.

Chief among the explanations given for suffering is that it is the consequence of our sinfulness or the sinfulness of others. We can see how very true this is. We are surely responsible for much of our own unhappines. We bring it on ourselves. We inflict it on others and we are also burdened by their failings. Anger isolates us; envy eats away at our hearts; self-pity deprives us of joy. Suffering is frequently the fruit of human sinfulness.

In those situations where we appear to be innocent of wrongdoing, we must look elsewhere for an explanation of our distress. It is then that we remember Abraham or Job and wonder if perhaps God is testing us as they were tested. It may be that we are being called upon to prove our obedience, our faithfulness, our trust in God. Understanding their plight in this way has helped many people to endure their suffering without being overpowered by it.

There are still other times when we view hardship as a kind of discipline sent by God, an opportunity for personal improvement. It is the fire that gold must endure if it is to be pure; it is the training that an athlete must undergo in order to be strengthened. It is the entrance into spiritual trans-formation.

Yet another way of interpreting one's adversity is to see it as a kind of vicarious affliction. We submit ourselves to it in place of and for the sake of others. We take upon ourselves their pain and sometimes their guilt in hopes that they will benefit from our suffering.

These are but a few of the explanations given for the hardships that accompany every life. Each of these has found expression somewhere within the sacred scriptures, particularly within the wisdom tradition, that tradition which originates from soul-searching reflection on the fundamental questions of life. These are explanations that have supported people in their struggles, have helped them to find some meaning in what appears to be meaningless, and have enabled them to rise above what might otherwise have held them down.

NONETHELESS. . .Not one of these explanations has adequately answered the question, Why? Why should a compassionate God inflict punishment that seems so far out of proportion to the wrongs of which we may be guilty? Why should innocent people suffer at the hands of the wicked especially when it appears that the really guilty ones are prospering from their sin? On the other hand, to claim that suffering is a test does not explain why the individual should have to be tested in the first place. What is gained when a weak human being is stretched to the breaking point? Is it not possible to develop as a person of integrity through times of honest soul-examination as well as loving social interaction? Why must one be wretched in order to be better? Besides, we all know that there is no guarantee that hardship and distress will mellow us, making us sensitive and understanding. The reverse might be true. We can harden in our bitterness and anger toward the world and everyone in it. Why should God place us in such jeopardy? Finally, is divine righteousness so fragile, so demanding, that it must be recompensed for even the slightest infraction regardless of who pays the price? Does this explanation really address the question, Why?

To challenge the inadequacy of these religious responses is not to reject them. Their greatest value may well be in their ability to provide support for people in their troubles, to enable them to rise above what might otherwise hold them down. They may not answer the question, Why? but they do address the question, How? One response exhorts us to suffer in such a way as to learn from our mistakes. Another encourages us to hold fast in obedience, in faithfulness, in trust, despite the hardships we may have to undergo. A third urges us to endure what cannot be avoided in order to give birth to patience and an understanding of human vulnerability. Finally, we may be inspired to commit ourselves and our suffering to the well-being of others. It can be a way of expressing our belief in the oneness of all people. We will have to look elsewhere for an answer to the Why? of suffering.

EVIL

We have all known a force that seems to work against life's positive creative dynamics of growth and development and refinement. It breaks down what life seems to build up; it diminishes what life endeavors to increase. This force governs and gives rise to wickedness and sin. We have experienced its movement within our own lives and we have seen its effects in the lives of others. It is the power of evil.

Evil has been described as the absence of good, an emptiness that should be filled with virtue, or the lack of uprightness. However, there is a dimension to evil that is experienced as a sinister presence in our lives, occupying and dominating us. This evil is real: it is no illusion. It is sharp and harsh and deadly.

We may well admit that we will be secure, at peace and fulfilled only if we live in accord with our covenant with the natural world, with each other, and with God. Nonetheless, we experience an almost overpowering insidious inclination to defy the order and harmony that sustain us. We choose to live lives of imbalance, of isolation, of absolute independence, lives that can only harm and might even destroy us. It is as if there were two opposing laws within us, one opening us to all of the possibilities of which we are capable, the other repudiating the true limits of creaturehood and seeking to establish its own rules by which to live.

The active presence of this evil in our lives perhaps best explains why we sometimes totally disregard the natural laws. In one instance we seem driven by a desire for more and more; in another we choose a path that results in devastating deprivation. In either instance, we place in jeopardy the delicate balance that is so essential for well-being. Something within us constrains us to work against our own nature. At times it is ignorance; at times it is thoughtlessness. At other times, however, it is a propensity toward anger and violence directed either toward ourselves, toward others, toward the world, or toward God. This is not a case of experimenting in order to discover the limits of the natural world. Rather, it is a case of a person who has a certain sense of some of these limits, yet who either disregards them or pushes them beyond the limit in order to cause pain and harm. We endanger our own health through reckless living; we torture others by straining their endurance or by depriving them of necessities; we overtax the ability of our world to sustain us. In all of this we really are defying what can only be called the plan of God. This is the power of evil.

This evil is felt not only on the material or physical level but also in the world of social relationships. We have all suffered from and been guilty of the manipulation and exploitation of others. We have preferred failure to collaboration, isolation to cooperation. There seems to be something within us that resists discovering the dynamics of social harmony and living in accord with them. We have used our social structures, the very structures that are meant to create and enhance healthy community, instead to exclude, to marginalize and to banish each other. We act in this way knowing that it will undermine the stability of society. In all of this we defy what can only be called the will of God. This is the power of evil.

We would not be able to ignore the plan of God or to oppose the will of God were we not free. This is why some have claimed that evil originates within human freedom. Our choices for integrity, for God, could hardly be noble choices if we did not have the opportunity to choose against integrity, against God, as an alternative option. It would seem that evil is the risk that freedom must face in order to be authentic.

Others have insisted that the power and influence of evil are too intense and penetrating for it to have originated through a merely human agency. They attribute it to a superhuman autonomous reality known by many names such as Satan, Lucifer, the Devil, the Prince of Darkness. According to this view, from the beginning of time this power has been the archenemy of God and has been in unremitting conflict with God, using the world of human beings as its battleground.

This explanation may be a way of understanding what appears to be a fundamental or radical battle between good and evil, but it does not explain the origin of this evil force. If it comes from God, we are faced with the dilemma of a good God bringing forth an evil power that works against God's forces for good. If it does not come from God, we must look for its origin in another source of creation or in its own self-generating power, and then we are faced with the consideration of a fundamental dualism.

The presence and the active power of evil in the world is an undisputed fact; its origin remains a mystery. The human heart is the arena wherein the contest between good and evil takes place. At times our victory seems to be assured. At other times we appear to be outmatched or outmaneuvered. Pitted against principalities and powers, we cannot find within ourselves the means to withstand much less overcome its force. This is the power of evil.

As impossible as it may seem, its power is never so furious as to force us to open our hearts to it. It may bend us and twist us and even break us, but it cannot force us to open our hearts to it. We may be battered or crushed or pulled apart, but in those instances we are its victims not its allies. Evil may hold us prisoner, but it cannot make us an ally unless we decide in its favor.

The strength that we need to cling fast to what is good and what is right is the compassionate love of God. Our conviction that God wants what is for our good, and that God provides for our well-being, may be the only defense we have against the seduction of the fury of evil. However, this faith is all that we need to bring us through an agony which can lead to a profound transformation. We may discover that we are not protected from pain, but we are strengthened in the face of evil. The forces of evil, whatever their origin, are no match to the power of good as found in God. We may not understand why there is evil in the world, but we know it cannot force us to open our heart to it. It may appear to have conquered, but this is only an appearance or it is only temporary. The goodness of the compassionate God is greater than all.

PAIN

Pain is no stranger to human existence, but it is really not a mystery. Being made of the stuff of the earth and being governed by the same natural laws, we pass through the stages of growth and deterioration as does every other living thing. Energetic straining forward and eventual breaking down are common to all. We are not immune to excessive cold or extreme heat. Nor can we sustain serious injury. Like every other organism we require proper nourishment and the right balance between activity and rest. We become ill because of the way our bodies react to foreign bodies within us. All of these conditions follow the laws of nature, laws that we have begun to understand and to work with within the science of medicine. It is because of our power of consciousness that we often experience pain in the midst of certain natural processes. Just as evil is the risk that freedom must face, so it would seem that pain is the price we must pay for consciousness. We might be tempted to ask why things are as they are, but then "Does the clay say to the potter, 'Why have you made me thus?'"

Pain is a very natural though unwelcome ingredient of life and should be dealt with gracefully, that is, with integrity and with God's help. Pain and diminishment are part of the cycle of life. Our own pain and our own diminishment serve to remind us that we are not in control of life but are participants in it. They are opportunities for humble acceptance of human limitation, limitation that does not deny human nobility nor the fact that we are especially loved by God. It can mellow and soften; it can bring out gentleness and understanding. It can lead us to an admission of our dependence on others, especially on God. Pain dealt with gracefully shows that physical diminishment does not mean diminishment of spirit.

Every aspect of the human condition can be borne with dignity. Pain is neither a sign that we are favored by God nor is it an indication that we have been renounced. It is a mark of being human and in possession of consciousness. Knowing this and believing that our pain, like everything else in the created world, is in the gentle hand of a loving God, can give us the strength we need to trust this God and to go on with courage.

DESOLATION

Perhaps the heaviest burden of life is the experience of desolation. It is the feeling of being helpless and alone in a hostile world, a feeling that can terrify a vulnerable, fragile human being. Gone is the sense of belonging to a supportive people; gone is the sense of oneness with creation; gone is the sense of being cared for by God. Our defenses are as nothing and we stand stripped and abandoned with no place to hide and nothing to do but tremble. We are overwhelmed by a profound awareness of the transient and contingent character of our existence, and by the realization that ultimately we are alone.

There is no mistaking that everything in the material world is transient. Although some things may last longer than others, they are still subject to change and so their present form is impermanent. We too face this unstable existence, but we know it and it frightens us. In fact, our moment on earth is just that—a mere moment. Our life is like a breath; our days are swifter than a weaver's shuttle. There is so much to see and feel and taste, there are so many places to be, so many things to do, and there is so little time. And we know it and it frightens us. Even those sensations and experiences that we are able to enjoy come and go like fleeting wisps of promise but not of possession. We cannot cling to them for they disappear within our grasp and we are left with nothing but memory and frustration. And we know it and it frightens us. All we have is what we have become and even that is so fragile and so ephemeral that we become desolate.

In addition to this, the interconnectedness of the material world and the mysterious momentum that moves it forward are experienced as being very impersonal. Despite the fact that each strand of the network is dependent upon the next, the impairment of one will seldom arrest the progress of the whole. The life force will simply make the necessary adjustments and move on without that one. We see ourselves within this fabric of life and we realize that, while we are totally dependent upon it, it is in no way dependent upon us. We may enhance it but we do not govern it. We are circumscribed by it; we are subject to it; our well-being, our very existence hinges upon its ordering, but it will continue when we are gone. We are so vulnerable to impersonal forces. And we know it and it frightens us.

Realizing that our days are fleeting and that we are only held to life by a thin uncertain thread, we turn to others for encouragement and support. We look to them for the stability and assurance that we cannot find within ourselves. At times we are comforted. At other times they have nothing to offer us but their own frailty, or else our need is more than they can meet, or they are indifferent to our distress. There is nothing that can alleviate our anxiety and so we are desolate.

The precariousness of human existence is a fact that we live with. Nothing, no one, can give us the kind of stability we seek. However, we can find peace in the thought that we have been brought into this precarious existence by a loving design that has held us in the past, holds us in the present, and can be trusted for the future. Though our time is short and uncertain, we can savor every moment, reverence everything we touch, cherish those who make up our life, and gratefully entrust ourselves to the care of God.

We are loved with more tenderness than we can even imagine and we are cared for with a solicitude that is boundless. However, we are afraid because of the immensity of life and our own insignificance before it. But still, our anxiety will change nothing. It will only prevent us from being humbly grateful for having been brought forth in the first place. We do not suffer because the hand of God has touched us. We suffer because we forget that we are in the hand of God.

HENCE, as long as we enjoy the power of consciousness we will be subject to the stress that accompanies it. We will be stretched and we will be diminished; we will be overburdened and we will be deprived. We will know it and we will suffer. As long as we enjoy the gift of freedom we will be torn between options. We will be tricked and tempted and threatened by evil. It is a conflict that will never end and the enemy will meet us on unsuspected battlefields. We are truly vessels of clay and yet we have been entrusted with consciousness and freedom, powers that mirror the divine. If we have been deemed worthy of such wondrous gifts, surely God will not abandon us with merely the burden of their weight.

As we search for the meaning of our suffering, let us move beyond the image of a vindictive God. We can learn from Job that the righteous do indeed suffer and for reasons they do not understand. What is important to note is the possibility that they may never understand. Yet they—we—can cling to God in our uncertainty and anguish. God has not abandoned and will not abandon us. We can learn the very hard lesson that confidence in God may not restore us to our former peaceful state, but it will definitely transform us. We will be led to new insights into life and a new awareness of God. We will discover that nothing can separate us from the love of God. "Neither death, nor life, nor angels, nor principalities, nor things present, nor things to come, nor powers, nor height, nor depth, nor anything else in all creation." There we will find our stability, our security, our lasting peace. Perhaps in suffering, more than in anything else, we can stand open before God.

The Sting of Death

> The dust returns to the earth as it
> was, and the spirit returns to God who
> gave it.
>
> *Ecclesiastes* 12:7

One and only one thing is certain. We will all die. We know this, but as we plunge into the adventure of life we seldom see death in our immediate future. It frequently takes the death of another, a near-death experience, or serious illness to jolt us into a realization of its inevitability.

Everyone knows the story of the primal sin in the garden

and the fateful consequences of that act. Many have specu-
lated on what life might have been like had our first ancestors
decided in favor of God's law rather than against it. Perhaps
we would not have been subjected to the ravages of time.
Surely we would have been spared the agony that often
accompanies the thought of death and of death itself. But how
would we have passed from this life? Would it have been
similar to a peaceful sleep? And what of our bodies? Would
they have been subject to diminishment and decay or would
they have undergone immediate transformation? If only there
had not been sin, then there would not be death.

Death is often seen as something that happens to us almost
as if from an outside force. We become the prey of disease, of
violence or of accident. We want to know what caused it,
hoping that this knowledge will aid us in preventing such a
death from occurring in others. Perhaps the enemy can be
delayed, even defeated. We know, however, that in the end it
will have its way. We will all die.

BUT . . . The biblical tradition does not really view death as
something imposed from the outside. Death does not appear to
be an intruder. Rather, it is understood as a very natural
phenomenon, the final stage in the ongoing process of life. A
careful examination of the Genesis account shows that,
although the threat of death as punishment is part of the initial
injunction (Gen 2:17), the actual sentence passed after the
offense condemns the couple to a life of hardship *until* they die
(Gen 3:19). It is only in a much later period of history, when
early Judaism had to contend with the influences of Greek
thinking, that the notion of original immortality appears in the
biblical writings. As oppressive as death may be, it is as natural

to us as are growth and development, diminishment and deterioration, and the early biblical traditions acknowledge this. It was not death but the circumstances surrounding death that created anxiety and challenged the faith and trust of the people.

UNTIMELY DEATH

Everyone hopes for, indeed expects to enjoy, the full cycle of life that reaches from the innocence and wonder of childhood, through the exuberance and daring of youth, into the fruitfulness and refinement of maturity. Then, in the final years, one can look back with satisfaction and pride and face death with a sense of peace and fulfillment. If the unfolding of life is arrested at any point, we feel cheated and we grieve for what might have been. We speak of people dying before their time. In this we are in agreement with our biblical ancestors who believed that a long, fruitful, happy life was the reward for living in accord with God and with the world. On the other hand, failure to achieve and enjoy the happiness that was expected at each stage on the journey through life was then and is now often viewed as either a punishment for sinfulness or else as the working of an unfair God. We feel that we have been faithful and, therefore, we have a right to a full complement of years.

What is a full complement of years? 70? 80? Is there some specific age that we can expect to reach? And if we do not reach it, is it right to say that death is untimely? Is fulfillment *in* life and *of* life primarily in the attainment of one's goals, the first of which is long life?

It is life and the way we understand life that determines how we view death. We want so much out of life, much more than we will ever be able to achieve. It is our insatiable desire for more, for everything, for God, that constrains us to set our sights on the future. No single moment, no point in time, can contain everything we crave and so we look to tomorrow and to years of tomorrows for the fulfillment of our dreams. When this prospect is withheld and we seem to be denied the time to achieve our goals, we speak of death as untimely and we struggle with the thought of the unfairness of it all.

It is life in the present that is of greatest value, not some happiness in the future. All we really have is now and the possibilities of this moment. True, some may not be able to survive the despair with which they are burdened without clinging to the hope of a better tomorrow. Even then, the hope is in the present; its possible fulfillment is in the future. Life must be lived, not merely charted. It must be entered into, not merely observed. We can drink deeply only of what we have; we can embrace only what is within reach. The gift of life is bestowed moment by moment, and that is how it is to be lived if we are to be filled with its delights. Just as we can cherish the past and yet not return there, so we may plan for the future but cannot live there. The wise Ecclesiastes insists that, since there is no guarantee that we will be able to accomplish our goals, and even if we do there is no guarantee that we will then be content, we should enjoy life as long as we live for that is God's gift to us. (Ecc 3:12f).

Life is in God's hands. Time is in God's hands. The way we commit ourselves to life and to the moment-by-moment living of it is in our hands. Some would say, It's all we have! Still, what a treasure even this is. It is a treasure we risk overlooking if all we do is fix our gaze on what will be, or rather, on what might be. A life that is savored in its own time, regardless of how long or how short this is, is far more meaningful and fulfilled than one that looks to the future for its realization. Death is always untimely, inopportune. But it would also be tragic if when we come to die we would find we had not lived at all.

SEPARATION AND LOSS

The thought of death, our own or the death of a loved one, is laden with the inevitability of separation and loss. An entire lifetime is spent knitting our lives with the lives of others and absorbing the sounds and smells and experiences of the world. And then, in one moment, this is all changed. The people to whom we looked for understanding and support, the very ones who shared our dreams and gave meaning to our strivings, are gone. We seem to have lost our bearings and are adrift with no familiar landmarks in sight and no assurance that we will be able to set a new course. Or else we dread the thought that we too will someday leave all that we have loved. The sense of separation and loss is one of the sharpest pangs occasioned by death.

When we love another and allow ourselves to be loved in return, we bring to birth a new reality, a relationship within which each partner lives and develops and comes of age in ways never before known and never to be repeated. This union is vibrant with the dynamic energies of each person. Then death intrudes and puts an end to this singular interaction. Gone is our dialogue partner and gone is our life-giving and life-enriching exchange. We have lost for all earthly time someone and something that gave special meaning and purpose to existence. While this particular love may not have been the only relationship in our life, it was unique and irreplaceable, it cannot be continued with another partner, and it will never be duplicated. Something very real has been severed. Its measure and significance in our life will determine the extent of the separation and loss that we experience.

What is true with regard to the death of another is similarly true with regard to our own death. We dread being snatched from the tender embrace of love and having the door to the future closed to us. We want life and love and all of the possibilities of each to continue to unfold before us. We do not want to leave the people or the world that are so much a part of us.

Each night we close our eyes in sleep, but always trusting that we will see a new dawn. We know that someday this will not be the case. Then we will close our eyes for the last time. Or if they do open again, it will be to a different world. Then again, perhaps it will be to the same world but a different dimension of it. It is this uncertainty, this great unknown that frequently frightens us. We who try to comprehend and to control every aspect of life are confronted by the great unknown and uncontrollable reality of death.

Once again we are brought face to face with the complex nature of human existence. We attach ourselves to life and to people in that life with a tenacity that defies separation, and we do this knowing that at any moment the cords of life can unravel and our whole existence can come apart. It is almost as if we refuse to accept death as the end of everything in life. It may appear to have the last word, but those words we did utter before it silenced us can echo in the hearts of the people who heard them and we can live on in memory. Love is stronger than death.

We are fascinated by the unknown. Our insatiable desire to understand it is the motivating force behind our never-ending search for knowledge. We seem able to venture out into the unknown as long as we can be assured of some hold on the secure and familiar. Death deprives us of any sense of security. We watch others slip away from us, never to return. We have no clue as to what, if anything, lies beyond. There is no way for us to retrieve what has been lost or to be retrieved when it is our turn to die. The unknown that so captivates us will eventually encompass us.

We are able to survive and to find pleasure in life to the extent that we can achieve a certain amount of control. This does not necessarily mean mastery. We learn to maintain things in balance and to live in harmony. Life teaches us this necessary lesson. Death, on the other hand, forces us to relinquish our hold on everything. We are as powerless when we leave the world as we were when we entered it.

The death of another leaves us bereft of our love, fully vulnerable in the face of the unknown, and completely powerless before what we cannot control. We do not really leave the world as we entered it. At birth we did not know love or security or control. Now we do and we must surrender our hold on them. We will be able to do this with a certain amount of peace if we believe that everything is in the hands of a loving, compassionate God.

We did nothing to bring life into being. It flows out of, and within, and back into, divine mystery. We are privileged to partake in its wonder, and in that moment we come to know and love others who are also tasting their moment. Like us, they belong to and are tenderly cared for by God. Although with their death we do experience the pain of separation and loss, we are not totally separated from our loved ones; they are not completely lost to us. Those who influence us, live in us, not merely because of memory but because they have fashioned us in ways that will endure. The greatest expression of our love for them and their love for us is the faithfulness with which we manifest their artistry in our lives. Then trusting in God, we entrust ourselves and them to God's safekeeping.

Death is not the great unknown or the ultimate reality that is beyond our control. God is. Death is rather the final invitation to abandonment to God's immensity and incomprehensibility. Throughout life we have had countless opportunities to trust in God, but nothing in life can compare with the step we will have to take at death. We can take this step with confidence for, while the reality of God has always been an unfathomable mystery, the traces of God that we have glimpsed have always been prodigal in their generosity, merciful in their understanding, and passionate in their loving-kindness.

LEAVING NO TRACE

Try as we may to ignore, even escape death, we know that this is impossible. Despite our remarkable successes in prolonging life, we cannot hold out against the inevitable. Ours is a culture that places a high value on the individual person and on that person's self-perception. "Know thyself" and "To thine own self be true" is advice that we have taken quite seriously. Our impressions of the world and of others are filtered through the prism of our self-awareness. Consciousness is our unique way of being in the world. It is not surprising, then, that we instinctively resist the thought that our death will not only put an end to earthly life, but it may well even completely obliterate every trace of who and what we were. It will be as if we had never even existed. Such an idea is hard to endure.

We want to leave our mark on the world, not necessarily an ostentatious mark but some trace of our own uniqueness, of our contribution to the flow of life and of meaning. Human reality and expression shine forth through each of us in ways never to be duplicated. What a loss if death should have the power to erase all of this.

Can it? Is everything really lost with death? Can we not say that the very continuity of life and the variety of its display are evidence of the contribution of scores of individuals? Would we be here, knowing all that we know, achieving all that we achieve had it not been for those who preceded us? The life force that surges through us and the human accomplishments that we call culture have been passed down through people little known or not remembered. They will be passed on by us, also people little known or not remembered. Perhaps our names will not survive on plaques or our features on the faces of others, but our influence can be felt in other lives. The clear blast of the trumpet does not alone make a symphony. Gentle strings and muted woodwinds are just as important even though not as pronounced. It is the entire composition that survives and it does so because of its rich and intricate harmony and balance.

At those times when the proportions of the world overwhelm us and we are despondent because of the transitory nature of our own existence, we can remember that we are an important part of the whole. The very possibility of a future and the richness of character depend upon the present, of which we can be a very vital part. Every person born is significant; every life makes a difference and leaves a mark. Nothing, not even death, can alter this.

HENCE, we will have to learn to spend less time fearing and avoiding death and more time loving and enjoying life. This is not to deny our apprehension. The specter of death will always be just out of sight, ready at any moment to step foreward. But it cannot claim us. Death has no dominion over us, or over anything for that matter. It is life that has the power and vitality; it is life that cannot be restrained. We are brought into it and we move out of it as if on waves against the shore, waves that empty themselves of all of the riches of the deep, then retreat in order to gather new strength, and once again rush forward with a rhythm that is constant yet never the same. The forces in this ebb and flow of life may appear to be impersonal, but they are not. Manifested through us, vital living beings that we are, they are *very* personal. They can be trusted. That is why we can live as fully as possible the moment-by-moment existence that is ours and leave the future to God. A single wave cannot determine the rhythm of the sea; it is an expression of that rhythm. An individual cannot direct the forces of life; it is a manifestation of those forces.

We know that life and death are not in our hands but in God's. The only way that we can be at peace with this fact is with confidence in God's care and compassion. The only way

to face death is with a passionate love for life and an uncondi-
tional trust in God.

We Hope for What We do not See

The souls of the just are in
the hand of God,
and no torment will ever
touch them.
In the eyes of the foolish
they seem to have died,
and their passing away was
thought to be an affliction,
and their going from us to be
utter destruction;
but they are at peace.

Wisdom 3:1-3

This life can be such a disappointment! We set goals for
ourselves, noble goals of self-improvement and the development and enrichment of society. We work toward these goals
and sacrifice ourselves for them and, more often than not, we
fail to see their accomplishment. When we are fortunate
enough to attain them, they either do not endure or we soon
weary of them. Everything we work for is so vulnerable, for
moths and rust consume and thieves break in and steal. It is as
if our life, our world, all creation is subjected to futility.

Life can be not only frustrating but also degrading. It can
prey on our weaknesses and tempt us to choose a path devoid
of integrity. It can strip us of human dignity and cast us aside
as refuse. It can grind us down to the dust from which we
came and leave us pleading for the release that death would

bring. Life has been aptly described as a "vale of tears."

The keen realization of the inadequacy of life along with profound confidence in the goodness of God combine to produce in us the conviction that death is not the end of all. Religious traditions throughout the world have had to deal with this issue and each one has devised its own way of giving expression to its beliefs. The biblical tradition embodies various perspectives on this question. As we ponder in particular the possibility of immortality or the resurrection of the body, the hope of some definitive and lasting retribution, we frequently move from a realization of the inadequacy of life to a disdain of it. When this happens, the real value of life is thought to be in its ability to prepare us for the life to come. We are urged to set our hearts on an afterlife where neither moth nor rust consumes and where thieves do not break in and steal.

EVEN SO . . . The source of our dissatisfaction with life frequently is the boundlessness of our desires and the unattainability of our goals. It is not that life offers us little or nothing; it is that we want more from it than it is able to give. We seek absolute fulfillment; we crave complete satisfaction. We are restless in our yearnings, yearnings that reach for something far beyond the experience of life. We will never rest until we rest fully in God. The limits of our life, the very limits that direct us and enable us to throw ourselves into the adventure of earthly existence of space and time seem to stand in the way of total union with God. And so we turn with total openness, not so much to an undisclosed hereafter as to the unfathomable yet faithful God.

EMPTY PROMISES?

In one sense it takes so little to make us happy—the feeling of well-being when our physical needs have been met, when we know that we are accepted and appreciated, when we look to our accomplishments with pride. We say that life has been good to us. In reality we may think that we have been good to life and that we are deserving of our good fortune. But when we encounter a setback or have to live with adversity, when the little that we ask is denied us, we are frequently thrown into confusion. How unfair it seems to have been brought needy and defenseless into a life that does not even provide us with the bare necessities. Surely the very order of the universe demands that we be sustained.

The biblical tradition is very clear in its insistence on righteous living and its attendant promise of reward. While it may change in its perception of what constitutes righteous living, it is unwavering in the principle. The notion of the justice of God rests on the conviction that God will guarantee happiness and fulfillment for the virtuous and will mete out appropriate punishment for the wayward. Since the justice of God was held to be the principle of cosmic order as well, the fate of human beings was related to the structure of the world. Surely the very order of the universe demands that we be compensated.

If God is good and God is just, and we are not sustained and we are not compensated, it is no wonder that we look to an afterlife, to another place where all things will be in proper order. Perhaps hope in such a future is necessary if we are to live at peace with this less-than-perfect present.

Our faith tells us and our experience has shown us that we never quite know what to expect from God or how to understand God's justice. At times we deceive ourselves thinking that we have discovered the mysterious pattern or divine plan. Then we are disappointed when things do not unfold as we thought they would, or should. We are faced once again with the limitations of our creaturehood. We can understand neither God nor life, much less control them. What we can do is believe in their promises, open ourselves to them, and trust that somehow, in ways we cannot even imagine, these promises will be kept. God does not deceive us, neither does life, and their promises though obscure are far from empty.

HUNGRY FOR MORE

We seem to have an insatiable appetite for what is beautiful, an unquenchable thirst for what is noble and true. We are charmed by these qualities, captivated by their excellence. We detect traces of them in people, in events, in the natural world, and in ourselves, and we are drawn to them openheartedly. Our desire to possess them could well be a desire to be possessed by them. Perhaps then our yearnings would be assuaged. But will this ever really happen while we are confined to the here and now?

It is true that being here enables us to drink deeply of all the wonders that surround us. Yet, being *here* hinders us from bathing in the splendor that is *there*. We want both; we want all. But we must choose, and our choice will always leave us with still more longing and a longing for more.

The time in which we find ourselves is our time. These are

"the good ole days." We have been shaped by the insights and perceptions and values of this era. We understand it. We live in the present and it is in the present that we experience the gentle care and compassion of God. Now is the acceptable time; now is our day of salvation.

Although we live in it, the now is still an elusive time. We do not know whence it comes, but it is always upon us and always original, and then it vanishes in deference to another now. There are moments that we treasure, moments of profound emotion that have joined us for all time to the people of our lives and the world in which we live. There are moments when we seem to have been swept away from the events around us into the timelessness of God. These are moments we cling to, moments we do not want to watch recede into the past where they cease to be *now* and are consigned to be *then*. We have no choice when it comes to time; we must live in the present, a present that cannot realize all of our possibilities.

As we ponder life in the here and the now, we begin to perceive the enormous discontinuity between what we desire and what we can achieve. Our longing seems infinite while our attainment is qualified. We identify this longing as an intrinsic desire for God who alone can fill us to overabundance. Although the finite character of our experience precludes the achievement of this goal, we cannot believe that we have been created for frustration. Surely there will be some way that God will bring us to fulfillment and we will be enraptured by the God for whom we long.

STRONGER THAN DEATH

Any thought of life after death presupposes that this life will entail some form of consciousness. If we were not conscious beings we would not be concerned with questions of retribution or of fulfillment. It is this eminent capacity that sets us apart from the rest of creation and endows us not only with powers but also with responsibilities. It is not likely that the afterlife will find us to be less than we are now.

The primary focus of consciousness is the here and the now. However, it is also a kind of organizing principle that brings together the operations of memory and imagination. In our memories we store up the treasures of the past which sometimes flood our consciousness and carry us back with them into cherished bygone times. It is with the imagination that we create new worlds with limitless possiblities that might take concrete form in the future. Our mental faculties are marvelous and they allow us to escape, if only in a small measure, from the confines of space and time.

There are other ways that we transcend these limitations. Our dreams and our aspirations not only fill our minds and hearts but themselves expand into dimensions that cannot be restricted. Already in this world we sometimes move beyond the level of matter-of-fact existence. We dare to hope that this would continue in some way after death.

What can be said about the vitality and transforming nature of love? We do not relinquish our attachment to people when they die. Although they may no longer play an active role in our lives, the bond of love remains and continues to influence us. Death has no dominion over love.

THEN, we are not foolish if we refuse to accept the finality of death. Our experience of life gives us indications of some kind of continuity. We have been made to aspire after the divine. Because this life does not seem to provide for the complete realization of that aspiration, are we to give up all hope?

We have no certitude about anything after death. What we have is hope. Hope that we will finally attain the wholeness for which we search. Hope that we will rest in the peace for which we long. Hope that we will be held by the God who calls us in life and in death.

We will surely die. There is no way of escape; this reality is out of our hands. We do have a say about the attitudes with which we face death. The way to die is really the way to live. We must learn to be open and trusting. We must love life with a passion that cannot be extinguished. As we do this, we must always remember that everything has been given to us by God whose tenderness cannot be imagined. At each moment we are held in the protective hand of God. Nothing in life can alter this. How could death bring it to an end?

I Place My Trust in You

> The righteous live forever,
> and their reward is with the
>   Lord;
> the Most High takes care of them.
>
> *Wisdom* 5:15

A life of prayer is a life spent in openness to God and to reality. It is a life of embracing the world and the people of the world with a devotion that mirrors the love of God. Everything we do and everything we are turns toward the radiance of God even as the flowers look to the sun for warmth and growth and approval. Just as the energy of that sun enters the flowers and effects the wonders of life, so we are filled with the mystery of God and we live a life called prayer.

Prayer and openness are the same. Both presume trust and acceptance. Both welcome the charm of the moment without closing the door to the wonders that might follow. We are born with such receptivity, such hospitality toward all. We must not lose it regardless of the real or imagined dangers that we face in a lifetime. If we do lose it, how can we pray? How will we live? And how will we die?

It is in the world that we learn to be open to life and to God. It is in the world that we learn to trust and to accept even when we know that suffering and death lie ahead. It is in the world that living teaches us how to pray. It is in the world, a profoundly prayerful place.